# G (

# PREACH THE KINGDOM
# HEAL THE SICK

*by*

*Jim Wilson*

*Foreword by John Townroe*
*Warden of King's College, London at*
*St. Boniface College, Warminster*

JAMES CLARKE & CO., LTD.
CAMBRIDGE

*First published* 1962
*Second impression* 1964

© THE GUILD OF HEALTH

Reprinted 1979

This book I dedicate to my wife
Norah who has assisted, inspired
and encouraged me in all my
work for o v e r fifty years.

David Green (Printers) Ltd, Kettering, Northamptonshire

# CONTENTS

# FOREWORD

Father Jim Wilson has visited King's College at Warminster every year since 1952 to give a course of lectures. The sessions for questions and discussion have never failed to produce most lively debate, though I have noticed in recent years that the audience seems more prepared in advance to receive much of his teaching, as if there were a movement of thought gaining strength in this country. I have noticed also that the lectures have been more and more successful in taking the accent off Health and Healing in themselves, and putting it on God and His Glory and His plan of renewal for the whole world. The danger of worshipping the god of health has been avoided, and the vast scope of Christianity has been revealed in its grandeur.

The lectures have led to the writing of this book. It contains, I believe, the message which God has given a priest to deliver to the Church today. But it is not a message which can be given in a single sentence. It will be necessary to read the whole book and the book as a whole, to gain both the true proportions and the full impact of this piece of modern Christian prophecy.

On the human level alone, this book is a remarkable achievement. Father Jim Wilson, who is eighty-one years old and has fifty-eight years in the ordained Ministry behind him, writes here with a masterly simplicity which will surely help everyone to hear what he has to say. By the grace of God, everyone who approaches it with an open mind will be enabled to hear also what it is that the Spirit here says to the Church.

The Christian prophet sees into the needs of the world around him, and discerns how distorted human life has become. He sees, too, that the Church of God in the world is under judgment for having failed to preach and embody God's Kingdom as it might have done. Having seen into the situation by faith, he can speak out from faith in Christ who alone can restore His world. "Scripture says, 'I believed, and therefore I spoke out,' and we too, in the same spirit of faith, believe and therefore speak out . . ." (2 Corinthians, 4, 13. N.E.B.). This is what Father Jim has done.

There are parts of this book which show not only the prophetic, but also the pioneering spirit. This is nothing new for its author. As his brother, Dr. Edward Wilson, made the adventure to the South Pole with Captain Scott, so Father Jim has often in his ministry shown the spirit of adventure for Christ's sake. He was, for example, a pioneer forty years ago of what is now widely known as the Parish Communion and the Parish Meeting.

In this book, Father Wilson can be found exploring the new knowledge of psycho-somatic medicine, and seeking to use it correctly in the Ministry of Healing. Some may have much to add, or even to modify, in these sections; just as others may be stirred to argument and fresh thought in the more technically historical and theological sections. This is what a pioneer wants, that others should go deeper into the country he has entered. If his maps need corrections at any points, he will be eager to have them made. But the fact remains that Father Jim Wilson has here brought matters to the attention of Christians which they will ignore at their peril.

Warminster, February, 1962.

JOHN TOWNROE.

Warden of King's College, London.

at St. Boniface College,
Warminster.

# PREFACE

For several years I have had the opportunity to conduct a week of teaching on the Ministry of Healing in a large Theological College. This book is based on this course. It has been thoroughly discussed and I have learned much myself by other peoples' contributions. I have also had forty-five years of experience in the use of this ministry, mostly in large industrial parishes. This does not mean that I know all that is to be known about healing. What I am convinced about is that Christ meant His Church to be the instrument through which He would continue to heal, not only sickness and disease, but the ills of the whole world; and that healing results wherever the life of God's Kingdom comes into expression. That is why preaching the Kingdom of God must precede healing the sick. Our Lord's teaching about the Kingdom was the good news or " Gospel " which He came to bring and where it is not preached, no Gospel is preached at all. The condition of the world today is the direct result of our neglect to preach the Gospel, because without it mankind is blind to God's purpose for the world. In this sense this book is a challenge to the Church. Unless we are prepared to repent and preach " the Gospel " and make the Church a fit instrument for God to use for His purposes of healing and redeeming and salvation, we will be swept away and salvation (healing) will come from elsewhere in the world.

I have tried to write in simple language for very ordinary people and I hope the book may be useful for discussion in groups. If in reading it God gives you a glimpse of what the Church could be and do; then may He give you courage to put what you see into practice for His glory.

JIM WILSON.

Edward Wilson House,
26 Queen Anne Street,   W.1.

# CHAPTER I

## THE WAY OF THE LORD
## THE PEOPLE OF GOD
## A HEALING COMMUNITY

The Ministry of Healing is seen most truly and clearly, not as a separate activity within the Church, conducted by " Healers " or people with special gifts but as the normal activity of God through Christ as it has been revealed to us in the whole Jewish and Christian revelation given to us in the Bible and in the Church.

The Bible is the story of what God has done and is doing now and of how He has made known His will and purpose to men. It is, in the Old Testament, a record of His dealings with a particular community. They are " the people of God," the Israelites or Jews.

History begins with the call of Abraham (Genesis 18. 17-19). "And the Lord said, shall I hide from Abraham that which I do; seeing that Abraham shall surely become a great and mighty nation and all the nations of the earth shall be blessed in him? For I have known him, to the end that he may command his children and his household after him, that they may keep the way of the Lord, to do justice and judgment; to the end that the Lord may bring upon Abraham that which He hath spoken of him."

This is one of the most revealing pronouncements in the whole of the Bible. First, because we are told that there is "A way of the Lord " and Abraham is called to walk in it. It means that God is at work in the world with a purpose which was working out even before man was called to share in it: and it is a purpose in which all the nations of the earth are to share and to find blessing.

Secondly, " to walk in the way of the Lord " means living in such a way that God's righteousness, that is, His justice and His love, will be expressed not only in a person's individual life and character but in all the social

7

life of the nations. So, Abraham is called to teach his whole family how to live in this way, for the sake of those who will follow them. In all this we have the key which unlocks a great deal of the mystery of the Bible and of the Christian Church and of the sacraments.

Abraham responded to God's call and taught his children to live " in the way of the Lord." They grew into a great nation in Egypt, but there they experienced slavery, not justice. But God knew of this. (Exodus 3. 7 and 10). "I have seen the oppression wherewith the Egyptians oppress them." God then calls Moses to lead them out of slavery that they may " walk in the way of the Lord " and experience righteousness. Moses then, in the wilderness, gave them the " Laws of Moses " which entirely aimed at teaching the nation to " walk in the way of the Lord." They were " the People of God " called to live in righteousness and there was to be no oppression (Exodus 22. 21-23): no money lending or usury (Exodus 22. 25-27): no slavery (Leviticus 25. 39-46): no permanent land tenure and therefore no exploitation (Leviticus 25. 8-17): and no unrighteousness or evil (Leviticus 19. 11-18). The nation of Israel was not chosen by God out of any favouritism but because they were responsive and thus able to be used by God for His purposes for the whole human race: because from the beginning of creation God has had the purpose of creating all things to be the means of expressing His own righteousness and thus bring His Kingdom into expression on earth.

Abraham realised this great truth. He believed that God was righteous, that is, that His character was that of justice and of love and that nothing would please God which did not express that character of righteousness. In believing this he grasped the great truth which came later to be known as sacramentalism, that is, that God always works to reveal Himself in creation: in other words that God is always working to incarnate Himself (see Chapter 19A). This is not pantheism, which identifies God and His Creation and thinks of it as part of God. We don't believe this; God is always different from us, always holy, always perfect spirit, and yet becoming incarnate or expressing Himself, and showing Himself, if we have eyes to see.

The Israelite nation settled in Palestine and tried to live up to the ideal set by Moses, to " walk in the way of the Lord." The whole history, then, of the nation is of this endeavour. Again and again they failed but always some great prophet of social righteousness arose to recall them to their ideal. Some of those prophets were loud in their condemnation of unrighteousness. (Jeremiah 4. 1-2; 5. 1; 7. 1-8, 21-26; 9. 1-3, 23-24: Isaiah 1, 1, 2, 3; 3. 13-15; 4. 8-9: Amos 5. 21-24: Zechariah 7. 9-11).

When they failed to amend their ways, disaster followed: yet in the midst of suffering there grew the hope that God would yet fulfil His promise: and they began to look for a Saviour sent by God to lead them into " the way of the Lord." (Isaiah 33. 13-17; 51. 7-8). They began to look for the coming of God's Kingdom with its righteousness (Isaiah 65. 17-25), and not only for healing and redemption of the human race but of the whole creation, for nature itself is tainted and fallen from God's purpose and needs redemption (Isaiah 11. 1-10, 65.25). There were times when the nation got a glimpse of the perfection of God's purpose for them: under Solomon and Hezekiah and Simon Maccabees, when " every man sat under his vine and under his fig tree in peace and plenty and there was none to fray them," but the struggle went on right down to the Roman occupation seventy years before the birth of our Lord.

All through this long period, from Abraham to Christ, the People of God were a healing, redeeming stream; a long thin line of protest and prophecy, often almost overwhelmed by the evil of the world but ever looking forward in faith to " the day of the Lord " when Messiah would come " with healing in His wings " to overcome all evil and suffering and to complete God's purposes for men.

# CHAPTER II

## THE KINGDOM OF GOD

Jesus took up the teaching of the Prophets of the Old Testament and developed it in His teaching about the Kingdom of God. It was the main theme of all His teaching. It is "the Gospel," "the good news," which the Church was commissioned to teach; and the Church was to be the instrument which the Lord would use for the fulfilment of His purpose for the world, to bring "the Kingdom of God on earth as it is in Heaven." The idea that a day would come when God's righteousness would triumph on earth over all evil and God's purposes be fulfilled was not news to the Jews: it was their national and religious hope (Isaiah 65. 17 to end). When in Nazareth, Jesus read the prophecy from Isaiah 61. 1. "The spirit of the Lord is upon me because He hath annointed me to preach good tidings to the poor; He hath sent me to proclaim release to the captives and recovery of sight to the blind, to set at liberty them that are bruised, to proclaim the acceptable year of the Lord" (Luke 4. 18 and 19): He added, "Today hath this scripture been fulfilled in your ears." The Jews knew what He was talking about and they thrilled to His message. "They marvelled at the gracious words that fell from his lips" (Luke 4. 22). It was only when He enlarged the idea of the Kingdom to include people of other nations as well as the Jews that they turned against Him and tried to kill Him, for the Jews had narrowed the hope of the Kingdom and of its benefits to themselves.

Our Lord's message was that "The time is fulfilled and the Kingdom of God is at hand: repent ye, and believe in the Gospel" (Mark 1. 15). It is "in their midst" (Luke 17. 21 R.V. Margin). It has come upon them (Luke 10. 9). They are to seek it first with His righteousness (Matthew 6. 33) and it will then bring its blessings, which are not entirely spiritual; they will include very physical benefits, clothes, food, healing as well as righteousness and peace. In fact the physical blessings will be the by-products of the life of the Kingdom and of living in " the way of the Lord." So much is the Kingdom of God the very heart of the Gospel and the very kernel of Christ's teaching that the Gospel is stripped of its essential meaning without it. The real problem of evangelisation today is how to interpret the phrase " The Kingdom of God " into language which will convey the thrill of its meaning to a world which has lost all sense of purpose and of hope for the future. Before attempting this we must note the very close connection between THE KINGDOM AND THE HEALING MINISTRY OF OUR LORD.

Jesus speaks of the Kingdom of God as something which is well-known to His hearers. It needs no explanation, yet He took infinite pains to enlarge His hearers' ideas on the subject. St. John the Baptist, who was a cousin of our Lord's and had probably been brought up with Him and who had recognised Him as " the Christ " (John 1. 36) was now in prison. Jesus had not declared Himself to be the Messiah and so St. John sends disciples to ask Him, "Art Thou He that should come or look we for another?" (Matthew 11. 3). Our Lord's reply tells John what is happening. " Go and tell John, the blind see, the lame walk, the lepers are cleansed, the deaf hear, the dead are raised and the Gospel is preached to the poor " (Matthew 11. 4-6). John will know what all those " who looked for the consolation of Israeal " (Luke 2. 25) would know, that these were the signs which were to be expected of the Messiah. St. John the Evangelist speaks of our Lord's works of healing as " signs " (John 4. 48). In the first three Gospels they are spoken of as " Mighty works." They are the signs that the life of the Kingdom has come and God's mighty power is active in the world. " If I by the finger of God cast out demons, no doubt the Kingdom of God has come upon you " (Luke 11. 20). The works of healing are the mighty works done by the power of " the Christ " who is " the Eternal Life." St. John in his

First Epistle, 1. 1-14, gives our Lord that title. He says, " That which was from the beginning, that which we have heard, that which we have seen with our eyes, that which we beheld and our hands handled, concerning the Word of Life (and the life was manifested) and we have seen it and bear witness and declare unto you, the Life, the Eternal Life, which was with the Father." Jesus healed because that eternal Life, with all the power and quality of God's Life was active in Him triumphing over evil, sickness, disease and early death. The Kingdom of God was " at hand," it was present in Him, and His mighty works declared the fact. It was one of the main purposes of our Lord's teaching to give His disciples the faith which would enable them to use this same power and to teach them to know that it was available to them in response to faith: " I am come that they may have life and have it more abundantly " (John 10. 10). " God so loved the world (which He had made to be His Kingdom) that He gave His only begotten Son, to the end that all who believe in Him (as the Christ and the leader to the Kingdom) should not perish (as people were perishing through wars and oppression and sickness and disease) but have everlasting life," zoé aionion — the life of the Kingdom (John 3. 16). Our Lord's works of healing were not done as evidence of His divinity, they were the evidence that the life and power of the Kingdom was present in the Christ, the Messiah. When Jesus sent the seventy disciples forth upon their mission to prepare for His own coming, they are told to "heal the sick and to say unto them, the Kingdom of God is come nigh unto you " (Luke 10. 9).

When the twelve Apostles are sent out likewise they are told to " preach the Kingdom of God and to heal the sick " (Luke 9. 2) and they did so (Luke 9. 6). And when the disciples returned to tell him about their mission and a crowd gathered round Him in the desert where He had retired, Jesus did exactly what He had told His disciples to do: " He spake to them of the Kingdom of God and healed them that had need of healing " (Luke 9. 11).

Jesus was concerned to redeem the world and to renew

it on the lines of God's original purpose. The day has dawned, the power of the Kingdom is at work in Him and the signs of it are here to be seen in his works of healing (Mark 3. 20-30). "If I by the Spirit of God cast out devils then is the Kingdom of God come upon you" (Matthew 12. 28).

His purpose is to restore God's spoiled and damaged creation, to overcome evil and the effects of evil, in order that God's purpose may be accomplished, and His creation may become His Kingdom on earth as it is in Heaven.

Jesus was deeply conscious that His Father was at work in the world with an ultimate purpose of wholeness and perfection. "My Father worketh hitherto and I work" (John 5. 17), and that "hitherto" goes back to the beginning of creation. God has worked from the beginning, with a purpose. He has seen the end from the beginning and the end is to be the perfect incarnation of His own being in all its beauty and perfection in and through the whole Creation. And the Son, Jesus, ever works with the Father. "I and my Father are one" (John 10.30). "The Son doeth nothing but what He seeth the Father doing" (John 5. 19). "My work is to do the will of Him who sent me" (John 4. 34).

## CHAPTER III

### THE PARABLES

The teaching which Jesus gave is largely contained in the parables and in the Sermon on the Mount which is more likely to be a summary of His teaching than one sermon.

It is important to realise that out of thirty parables spoken by Him, twelve begin with the words "The Kingdom of Heaven is like." Twenty-one of the parables deal with the subject of the Kingdom and in twelve of them there is the idea of crisis. "The Day" will come when this age will end and the Kingdom come with judgment.

Only nine out of thirty parables fail to deal obviously with the subject of the Kingdom and are concerned with the way of life more generally.

The parables give different aspects of the life of the Kingdom. It will begin in a small way like the mustard seed (Matthew 13. 31 and 32), but it will grow and its life cannot be hid; it will encompass the world. There will be much seed wasted, as in the parable of the sower (Mark 4. 3-8), but the harvest will be sure. In some of its working it will be hidden, like the leaven in the dough (Luke 13. 20 and 21), but the whole world will one day be leavened. It is a treasure hidden (Matthew 13. 44-46) and yet when anyone finds it, it is like a costly pearl worth all that we have to give for it. It will not be at once a manifestation of pure goodness for, as it grows, tares are sown amongst the wheat (Matthew 13. 25) and only at the end will the pure goodness of the Kingdom be seen. The day will come when the good will be sorted out from the evil as in the parable of the draw net (Matthew 13. 47-50). Its growth is like that of the seed or of the vine, there will be need of our co-operation (Matthew 21. 1-16), we are called and sent to work in preparing for the final harvest and the fruit. We are called and sent into the vineyard to share in the work and we shall receive a due reward if we do our share and our best. But, many will reject the invitation as guests to the great supper for they (Matthew 22. 1-14) are too busy with their own purposes to care about God's: some will wait for the coming of the Kingdom without thought or preparation like the foolish virgins (Matthew 25. 1-13) and others will reject the opportunity given them like the man with the one talent (Matthew 25. 14-30). But all through the ages God cares: there is the lost sheep (Luke 15. 3-7) and the lost coin (Luke 15. 8-10) and the lost son (Luke 15. 11-22) and God ever seeks and forgives—for it is God's purpose to seek and to save that which is lost, for His purpose embraces the whole human race and the creation.

Our Lord was sure that the life of the Kingdom was present and at work in Himself (Luke 17. 21): that the

14

Kingdom has come and will soon be seen more fully. He could never have preached the Kingdom of God if he had not believed and expected that those He preached to would respond to His teaching. As time went on His disciples were slow to respond and opposition grew amongst the leaders of the nation and of the Temple, and Jesus began to realise that they were not ready and that they would reject Him. Thus His own conviction grew that the way of suffering lay before Him and that the Coming of the Kingdom would be delayed. Running through the Gospel there is therefore the two-fold expectation, of the immediate Coming of the Kingdom and of the delayed Coming in the distant future. When the Pharisees ask when does the Kingdom come? Jesus said, " The Kingdom of God cometh not with observation : Neither shall they say, Lo, here or, There ! for Lo, the Kingdom of God is in the midst of you " (Luke 17. 20, 21 R.V. Margin). And yet it was in the future because the power of evil must be broken and its evil results changed and much will depend on the response of those who have been called into fellowship with Christ in the cause of the Kingdom before God's purposes and will, can be fulfilled in the perfecting of creation and of the human race.

This was to be the work of the Church. The work of those, who like His disciples would be prepared to give themselves to His service and to take up the Cross with Him. So Our Lord teaches His disciples and sends them out on evangelistic journeys with the command to preach the Kingdom of God and to heal (Luke 9. 1-2). This is the Gospel—the Good News—that God is at work in the world not only creating it with a purpose of wholeness and perfection, but working to overcome all the evil which has spoiled and is thwarting His purpose; working to redeem the world from every evil and to heal all sickness and disease and even to restore to life those who have died prematurely from sickness.

This was the Good News (Gospel). Not, as it is often today that, if you go to Church and are good, you will go to Heaven when you die, but that God works: He loves the world which He has made: it is not His will that people should perish through war and sickness and other evil but that, working with Him to overcome evil, the world shall become His Kingdom in which all men will be able to experience LIFE in all its fulness, " Eternal Life." The thrilling good news is that this Kingdom is now at hand.

Those who went out with this message of Joy and hope for a fallen and hopeless world, believed that it was true and that God was at work; and being told to heal the sick as well as to preach they obeyed and " healed everywhere " (Luke 9. 6). It is this faith and this Gospel which needs to be recovered as the background to the Ministry of healing in the Church.

## CHAPTER IV

## JESUS TEACHING AND HEALING

St. Matthew tells us that St. John the Baptist began his teaching mission with the constant refrain " Repent ye: for the Kingdom of Heaven is at hand " (Matthew 3. 1-3): and that Jesus began His mission with the same words (Matthew 4. 17). After calling His disciples, He starts at once to travel about with them through Galilee, teaching in their synagogues and preaching the Gospel of the Kingdom and healing all manner of disease and sickness among the people. St. Luke fills in details of this healing ministry (Luke 4. 16; 6. 19).

Then follows the Sermon on the Mount (Matthew 5 and Luke 6. 20). The subject of His teaching is the Kingdom of God. " Blessed are ye poor: for yours is the Kingdom of God " (Luke 6. 20). He has not come to destroy the Law of Moses and the teaching of the Prophets but He does fill out and gives a fuller slant to all their teaching. Six times in St. Matthew's Gospel the refrain comes, " Ye have heard it said to them of old time . . . but I say unto you " (Matthew 5. 21, 27, 31, 33, 38 and 43). He came "not to destroy but to fulfil." It is here also (Matthew

6. 24 to end) that Jesus points to the activity of God's life in all creation, in the grass, the lilies, the birds and without making any distinction goes on to say "how much more shall He clothe you O ye of little faith." There is a wholeness in this teaching which is so much more Catholic in the true sense of that word (kath holos according to the whole) than that in which we have often been taught to think. We have been taught to think of there being a great division between the natural and the spiritual: instead of thinking of God at Work in all Creation: of God as "the Father, above all, through all, in all " (Eph. 4. 6).

Jesus taught us to see God at work expressing His life in an ascending scale, more and more fully in the whole creation. The Old Testament tells us that the "Holy Spirit brooded upon the face of the deep " (Genesis 1. 2), and brought order out of chaos; and the Holy Spirit has been active in all creation from the beginning in the whole process of incarnation, so that God is revealed in the beauty of a blade of grass and yet more fully in the lilies in the beauty of creation; and yet more in the birds and animals, in their beauty of song and in mother love: and quite consistently in the far fuller revelation in ordinary human beings in their capacity for fuller character and spiritual discernment, in their love and goodness and courage and forgiveness. But in perfect man and perfect human nature a still fuller revelation is given when God Himself is incarnate, fully in Christ. So the Holy Spirit has been working in all the world from the beginning, inspiring the prophets and speaking through them, revealing Himself in all creation, preparing "the way of the Lord;" responding to the prayers of Zacharias (Luke 1. 13); and working through St. John the Baptist; overshadowing the Virgin Mary and bringing "The Christ " into the world; and later, calling the Church into existence and filling it with his own life that it might be His Body in the world. It is the working out of this revelation of God Himself through His creation which is the whole meaning of the Kingdom of God; it is a process of incarnation. So God was revealed in the birth of Jesus; and in His childhood; and in all His character and work, in His healing of the sick and in the raising of the dead; and supremely in His sufferings at the hands of sinful men, on the Cross, overcoming evil by suffering not by punishing the sinner, thus ending its power. It is in the Cross and resurrection that God is seen triumphant over sin and evil through suffering.

It is in this setting that we see the place of Our Lord's works of healing. Here at work in the world was " that Eternal Life which was with the Father " (1 John 1. 2, 3), being manifested unto us in His true nature as Healer and Redeemer, overcoming evil and making whole. The works of healing were not spoken of as miracles but by St. John as "signs" (John 2. 11), and by the other Gospels as "mighty works " (Matthew 13. 58), or " works." The word which should be translated by the word miracle (terata) is used of the natural pagan healers whom Our Lord spoke of as " false prophets " (Matthew 7. 15-23; and Mark 13. 21). Our Lord spoke of His own healing work as manifestations of the Kingdom : " If I by the finger of God cast out demons, then is the Kingdom of God come upon you " (Luke 11. 20), and when the seventy disciples are sent out, they are told to explain their healing work by saying, " the Kingdom of God is come nigh unto you " (Luke 10. 9). Christian healing is the normal working of the life of the Kingdom of God called into action by faith in God. " The Son doeth nothing but what He seeth the Father doing " (John 5. 19). It is this simple faith in the living Christ active in the world today through His Body—the Church —which we have lost and need to recover for this is the faith needed in Christian healing.

It is into fellowship with Christ in this world-wide and timeless purpose of God that we are called by our baptism. As St. Paul reminds us, " Ye, the called of Jesus Christ " (Romans 1. 6). We are not called to save our souls for a future heaven but to give ourselves and all we have and are to God's purpose of making this world into His King-dom by challenging and overcoming sin and evil and by learning how to incarnate His life and character and thus to grow into true sonship to God, reflecting and expressing His character and living in such a way as will help forward His purposes of love and goodness for all mankind. This can best be achieved in the fellowship of the Church, for our Lord was the bringer of a Corporate Salvation. It is in and through the love of a community that we enter into Life.

## CHAPTER V

## THE CHURCH AND THE KINGDOM

The nature of the Church derives from the nature of God. It is not a man-made association or fellowship of men, gathered together by the act of their own wills, but a creation of God, a body, through which he purposes to work in His creative and redemptive activity in the world.

God's nature is that of community. The doctrine of the Trinity is an attempt to put this into words. We believe that God is Love, but love cannot exist by itself: it must go out in love and be responded to: it is an activity. So the Father, who is Eternal Love, loved and that which responded to His Love within Himself we call " the Son " or " the Word." The Son loved the Father and responded to or expressed the Father. And so the spirit of Eternal Love came from the Father to the Son, and from the Son to the Father binding them into one Eternal Trinity in unity. Thus God's nature is an activity of love and community.

Creation is the extension of this activity of expression into time and space. God has created all things through the Son (John 1. 1-2), who ever works to give back to the Father a creation which expresses Him or worships Him : for worship is the response which the creature makes to the Creator. "All the earth doth worship Thee the Father Everlasting " (Te Deum).

The life and activity of God is always creative, working to create a universe which in every detail will reflect back to God something of His own perfection : but this purpose of God has been spoiled by evil, because from very early in the whole process of creation there must have been a misuse of some form of very elementary liberty or freedom, and creation itself fell short of expressing the glory of God (Romans 3. 23), and thus imperfection and disharmony came into creation, which later, only when man appeared, became moral evil and sin. Thus very early in creation came the need for redemption—the overcoming of evil that God's purpose of perfection—the Coming of His Kingdom—might be accomplished. And God who is always " in all as well as above all " (Ephesians 4. 6), took upon Himself the evil of the world, bearing it and triumphing over it by suffering it in Christ. This redemptive activity of God was shown to us in the Cross, it was part of the incarnation. There on Calvary was nailed the eternal word and expression of God. He was the Vine of whom every soul ever born into the world or to be born, were branches (John 15. 1-8), and on Him therefore was laid all the sin and evil of the world with all its resultant sickness, suffering and sorrow and there as the Suffering Servant (Isaiah 41. 8) He triumphed over it, not by punishing the sinner but by suffering: revealing God's true nature of love and redemption and forgiveness. In this triumph, the power of death was broken and Christ rose from the dead. The incarnation of God in Christ is only seen in its fulness when the suffering on the Cross, the entire redemption of all evil through suffering, and the deliverance of man from the power of death and evil, are seen in the Risen Christ in his resurrection Body. Here is seen " that Eternal Life which was with the Father manifested unto us " and it is this Life which is to be the Life which fills His Body the Church, which is to be triumphant over sin and evil, sickness and disease. It is the Life of God's Kingdom which is manifested on the Cross and in the resurrection, showing us the power of the spirit over flesh, a power which would again be manifested in the life of the Church through faith in the living Christ in His Body. For just as the Christ had healed the sick, raised the dead, walked on the water, fed the multitudes, stilled the storm by the power of that Life which was in Him, so He overcame all evil and death itself by His Cross and resurrection. The Kingdom of God was there in Him and He taught His disciples to believe that the same power was available to them through faith in Him. He came " that we might have Life and have it more abundantly." And yet it is just the faith which makes that abundant life available to us today that we have lost and which we need to recover in the Church, that the Church may heal as it was told to do.

The Church exists, then, to interpret the Kingdom of God to the world—" Go and preach the Kingdom of God and heal the sick " (Luke 9). It is to be the instrument or body which the Risen Christ will use for His purposes. It is the means of His continued incarnation in the world. The Church is not the Kingdom of God itself. The Roman Church has made a great mistake in teaching this and when people speak of bringing people into the Kingdom, meaning the visible Church on earth, or talk of the spread of missionary endeavour as " the extension of God's Kingdom," they are making the Church as the Kingdom an end in itself. The Church then becomes the centre and the circumference of the so called religious interests of those within it. So far then as members of the Church are interested in people outside the Church, it is only with a view to bringing individual souls into " the Ark of the Church." Their interests then as Church people in the affairs of the world are confined to defending the Church against any who threaten its security, its power, its prestige or its possessions. The Church becomes unconcerned about God's purposes for the world as a whole and in the end denies the truth that God works in history and is concerned with society as well as with individuals and even with the material world. The Church is not an end in itself. It is the healing stream within all life, carrying in itself the vision and foretaste of God's Kingdom, the way of life. It " is Christ " (1 Corinthians 12. 12); the power of God, challenging evil and overcoming it and giving new life to the world. Most significantly the

Church is spoken of in the Acts of the Apostles (9. 2, 16, 18; 19. 9; 19. 23; 24. 14; 24. 22) as "The Way" for it's life on earth prepares the way for the Kingdom which will be the completion of God's will and purpose for the whole creation. It is the way of the Lord into which Abraham was called. (Chapter 1.)

## CHAPTER VI

### THE CHURCH — THE BODY OF CHRIST

Jesus sent the Church into the world to preach the Gospel and to heal the sick (Mark 16. 15-18). The Gospel is obviously the good news of God's purpose for the world, contained in all that Jesus taught about the Kingdom of God (Luke 9. 2, 6). Unless the Church preaches the Kingdom of God it does not preach the Gospel at all. The Church is also sent to heal: and as the Church is the Body of Christ and a community it is the whole Body which is to heal and not special "healers." (On special "Healers" see Chapter XXII.)

Jesus spoke of Himself as the Vine and of us as the branches, and the life of the tree is in the branches. St. Paul taught people that the Church is the Body of Christ (soma). And using that word he really meant a body with unity amongst the members. The word soma could not mean a congregation or collection of isolated people or a collection of limbs. The Church was to St. Paul, Christ, in the continuation of His incarnation. "For as the body is one, and hath many members and all the members of the body, being many, are one body, so also is Christ" (1 Corinthians 12. 2). St. Paul had persecuted the Christian Church and at his conversion heard our Lord say, "I am Jesus whom thou persecutest" (Acts 9. 4). But it is in the Epistle to the Ephesians 5. 22-32 that St. Paul reveals his idea of the Church most clearly. Christ is "the head of the Church" which is His Body and "we are His flesh and His bones," and Christ is concerned that His Body shall be "without spot or wrinkle" or any defect, but holy and without blemish. Again "Know ye not that your bodies are members of Christ?" (1 Corinthians 6. 15) and in Hebrews 13. 3, " Remember them that are in bonds, as bound with them; them that are evil entreated as being yourselves also in the body." We are reminded in language such as this of the community feeling amongst the Zulus in South Africa who have a proverb, " If there is a thorn in the foot the whole body must stoop down to pull it out " and of the African in the Cape Province who does not say " My brother is sick " but " We are sick in my brother." There is a deep sense of corporate life in all this which we don't find in the modern Church. It must be recovered.

There is no doubt that St. Paul and the Early Church thought of the Church on earth in this corporate, community way. As the early Christians gathered together to worship God they formed the body through which Christ could worship the Father and thus they entered into His worship. Members of the Church who fell away were members of Christ's Body : and so were those who were sick. The prayers of the Church for them were expressing, not only its desire for their healing but Christ's concern that His Body should be without spot or wrinkle or any blemish. Their very flesh was part of His Body. In a jig-saw every piece is of importance — it has its contribution to make, and no other piece can take its place and if there are pieces missing the picture will be spoilt. This is why regular attendance at Church is important. Every member of the Church has his place in the Body and a contribution to make and should be taught to know his responsibility to Christ and to the other members for making up the Body of Christ as it gathered to worship. It will be said, quite truly, that this is too local and too materialistic an idea of the Church : but St. Paul also sees the whole Church, and not only the local Christian group, as the Body of Christ. In Ephesians 4 he sees all the members of the Church united in one Body of Christ attaining the unity of the faith and coming to " a full grown Man " and to " the fulness of Christ," " for there is one body and one spirit, even as we are called in one hope of our calling; one Lord, one faith, one baptism, one God and Father of all who is above all and through all and in you all."

We often ask, "What is our destiny after death?" Isn't it eventually to find ourselves as members of Christ, such as we were made at our baptism, in the place which he has prepared for us in that great community life which is the life of God in Christ and where we shall be in Him, as He told us: "I am in the Father, and ye in me, and I in you" (John 14. 20). That is God's purpose for us, a purpose for which we have to prepare ourselves, not only by becoming true sons of God and growing into His likeness, but by entering into fellowship with Christ and sharing in all the activity of His Body the Church on earth. Thus life in the Church militant here on earth, prepares us for membership in the eternal life of God as members of Christ's mystical Body, in which He will come again to earth, with His Saints, at the coming of His Kingdom.

If the Church is to do this a great deal of teaching will have to be given to our congregations who at present are content to come to Church as complete individualists, sitting row by row like acorns in a box, full of potential life and growth but content, not even to know the names of those who sit next to them, nor to have any consciousness of the world around, where Christ is being crucified every moment by the evil and cruelty of the world and waits for a body through which He may speak of the purpose of His Kingdom and redeem the world. The worship of the Church should be giving people a vision of the world redeemed, its life should be a community life, giving a foretaste of the life of the Kingdom to those who take part in it. There will be an awareness of what is wrong with the world and a growing sense of the presence of the living Christ in the midst of the evil: a desire to stand aloof from the evil; and yet a growing sense of responsibility for working with Christ to put right what is wrong. Members of such a Church would learn to think and speak positively, aware of God's activity around them and of the unlimited spiritual resources which are in His life

24

within them.  A Church or congregation becoming aware
of Christ as He is, working in the world through His Body
in this way would soon become a healing Church, for
Christ Himself would be able to use their faith for His
purposes of wholeness and to manifest his Kingdom
through them in the world.


## CHAPTER VII

## THE EARLY CHURCH

We have seen what an enormous change will have to be
made in our whole idea of what the Church is and of
what our being made "members of Christ" in our
baptism means.  God is at work, redeeming the world,
there is a struggle and a fight going on in the world
between good and evil and we are united with Christ in
this fight.  We know His purpose and we are ready to
give ourselves, our souls and bodies to His cause, whatever it may cost us.  But is Christ in the world now? Isn't
God far away up in Heaven?  We have heard a great deal
about saving our souls for heaven and most of our modern
hymns seem to think that this is the whole purpose of
going to Church and of religion.  But no!  Jesus didn't
teach us to pray that we might get to heaven when we die.
He called us to help Him to clear up the evil of the world
and bring the Kingdom down from Heaven to earth.  " If
any man would come after me let him deny himself and
take up his cross and follow Me.  For whosoever would
save his soul shall lose it : and whosoever will lose his soul
for my sake shall find it.  For what shall a man be
profited, if he shall gain the whole world and forfeit his
soul?" (Matthew 16. 24-26).  And yet, and yet, how much
of our church-going is motivated by a desire to get something for our own benefit and how little idea of giving
there is.  Why do you go to Church?  Some will say, " I
have always been, it's a habit."  Others, " because I like
the sermons " or " I like the priest " or " I enjoy the

fellowship " or " I go with a friend " or " I like the sing-
ing " or the ceremonial or the simplicity or " I go for the
good of my soul."   How many people go to Church to
train themselves to take their part with Christ in what He
is doing now in the world?   But this means helping the
Church truly to be the Body of Christ in the world.
challenging evil and working to bring God's Kingdom
with its justice and fellowship on earth amongst men.   It
is a call to sacrifice and to giving, expecting no reward but
that of knowing that we do God's will.   It would be a
return to a Church life which would be much nearer to
the pattern of the Early Church

There were, in the Church in Apostolic days, several
characteristics which are notably absent from the Church
of our day.

1. The Church was in any particular place a fellowship.
   It was not just a church-going congregation but a
   koinonia or as St. Paul put it, " the Body of Christ "
   of which the members were " His flesh and His bones."
   There was a spirit of love uniting them so that if one
   suffered all suffered.   Those who were sick were sick
   members of Christ's Body and all the members were
   concerned for their healing.

2. The presence of the risen living Lord was with them
   always and they had perfect faith in Him and in His
   power.   St. Peter had no doubt that Jesus would heal
   the crippled man at the Beautiful Gate of the Temple.
   Jesus had sent St. Peter out with the Twelve " to
   preach the Kingdom of God and to heal," and he
   knew from experience that God would heal through
   them : He didn't say " look on Me," but " look on us."
   Though the people marvelled, St. Peter was not sur-
   prised : he says at once : it is by faith in the name
   of Jesus that he is healed, not by any power of " my
   own," or even "our own."

3. They preached Jesus " that He is the Christ " (Acts
   5. 42; and 9. 22).   Their message was the Gospel of
   the Kingdom and the leader to the Kingdom has come

and as St. John puts it, " That Eternal Life which was with the Father and which was manifested unto us " is now at work in the world through His Body, the Church, working to redeem the world. It is that Eternal Life which healed the sick, raised the dead, rose itself from the grave and stilled the storm, to which nothing is impossible today: " All power hath been given unto me."

4. It was this Fellowship or Body of Christ, so certain of the presence of Jesus and with such simple faith in His power and in His purpose for the world which challenged the life of the Roman Empire and brought persecution, which again brought deeper devotion to Christ. Is it any wonder that it healed the sick and brought new life and hope to millions and undermined the whole pagan society of its day?

How little of all this simple faith in God is character-istic of the Church of our day. But, unhappily, persecution did have its effect and little by little, as three centuries of persecution rolled on, much of this vivid faith fell away. It was not that persecution continued all the time: there were intervals of peace and growth but the Church was never popular and was always open to attack and it con-tinued till the early part of the fourth century when Constantine, the Emperor of Rome, granted toleration to the Church in 312 A.D. and persecution ceased.

During these early days of persecution, and also of struggle against every kind of heresy we hear of the ministry of healing being exercised as a normal part of the life and work of the Church. Justin Martyr, 163 A.D., writes about healing and exorcism brought about " by many of our Christian men." St. Irenaeus, Bishop of Lyons (180 A.D.) says that it is common knowledge that the Church has power to heal and tells of many cases of healing and even of raising of the dead. He speaks of the " laying on of hands " and of exorcism of evil spirits.

Origen (248 A.D.) refers in several places in his writings to the healing work of the Church and tells of cases of healing known to him personally. Besides these personal testimonies to the ministry of healing there is the evidence of the prayers and liturgies of the Early Church. It is clear that the blessing of oil and then annointing the sick for the healing of the whole person was a normal practice in the Church. It was all so normal that without the liturgies we might have had even less reference to it in the writings of the early Christians. But, it also seems to be clear that in the first three centuries, far too much reliance was placed in Christians who had natural gifts of healing and that this led to abuse and very gradually the ministry fell away into superstition, and we find extravagant stories of miracles and the custom of bringing people to the tombs of the Saints who had a reputation for healing, and healing by the use of relics, replacing the simple ministry by faith in the power of Christ through His Body, the Church. Though the ministry of healing probably continued in the Church, it ceased to be the centre of Christ's redeeming, healing work. Holy Unction became Unction for the dying, and the Roman Church today teaches that the Healing Ministry was withdrawn after the Apostolic age.

## CHAPTER VIII

### CHANGES IN RELIGIOUS THOUGHT

In the year 312 A.D. Constantine, Emperor of Rome, was converted to the Christian faith. He not only ordered persecution of Christians to cease but the Christian Church became the official religion of the Roman Empire. The conversion of Constantine was not such a blessing to the Church as we might have expected it to be. St. Cyprian tells us that after long persecution the Church had become corrupt. He speaks of pride, vanity, covetousness, quarrelling, intermarrying with the heathen: of Bishops becoming worldly and engaging in trade, of failure in simple faith and prayer, and of division in the Church.

In such circumstances the Church was hardly prepared for what was coming. The Church suddenly became the official religion of the Roman Empire, it became rich: it could hold property: it became popular. Crowds of pagans must have come for baptism. The Church was unable to absorb and teach so many. The result was that instead of the Church leavening the pagans, they leavened the Church's life. The result was that slowly but surely there came about great changes in the faith of the Church in the fourth and fifth centuries.

These changes are sometimes spoken of as "the great apostacy." And they have affected the life and witness of the Church for sixteen centuries and still do so. There were two main changes in religious thought and these brought great changes in purpose and organisation.


1. *Change in thought about God.*

Our Lord's teaching had emphasised teaching which was well based in the Old Testament, of God's life being active in the world and in all creation. The Holy Spirit had brooded upon the face of the deep bringing order out of chaos from the beginning. "Am I a God at hand, saith the Lord, and not a God far off? Can any hide himself in secret places that I shall not see him? Saith the Lord. Do not I fill heaven and earth?" (Jeremiah 23. 23).

Isaiah 6. 1-9 sees the Lord in His Vision high and lifted up, but also filling the Temple: it is the Lord who is worshipped in all His glory by the Host of Heaven of whom it is said, "The whole earth is full of His glory." There is no doubt of the immanence of the transcendence in Old Testament teaching, and our Lord strengthened it: "I am in the Father and ye in me and I in you" (John 14. 20). And in His teaching on the Holy Spirit (John 14), "Ye know Him for He dwelleth with you and shall be in you." And St. Paul is abundantly clear on this point. In Ephesians 4. 6, "One God and Father of all who is over all, and through all, and in all." His whole teaching is of God who is in Christ active in the world. In the

Sermon on the Mount the Holy Spirit is active on the natural level in the world.

What then happened, slowly but surely, to change the thought of the Church in the fourth and fifth centuries, so that God became thought of as someone who was far away up in Heaven, concerned not so much to change the world and to overcome evil and to bring His "Kingdom on earth as it is in Heaven;" as to save souls out of this world so that they might go to Him in Heaven when they die?

There is no doubt that this change did come about and that as a result the medieval system of the Church grew and was successful and is still successful and it survives in the Roman Catholic Church today. There are still many people outside the Roman Communion who defend that system as the normal faith and practice of the Church. But it was certainly a great departure from what was normal in the Church of the first three centuries. True Catholicism is free from dualism. The word "Catholic" consists of two Greek words, kath and holos, and means according to the whole. And a religion which teaches that there is a great division between God and creation or between nature and grace is not Catholic. In this sense the Roman Catholic Church is a complete denial of Catholicism. The argument was thrashed out in the first three centuries in Alexandria, and the names of St. Clement, Bishop of Alexandria and of St. Athenasius and Origen stand out in defence of the Christian faith and of the incarnation as revealing the truth of the kinship of the human with the Divine, for God is all and is ever working to incarnate His life in all, sacramentally. "The great apostasy" robbed mankind of the knowledge of the indwelling life of God's Holy Spirit which Jesus taught us. And the whole idea of God became different to that of the New Testament. We must face this fact and get back to the faith of the early centuries and of the Gospels.

## 2. *How did it all come to pass?*

We saw that when the Church was freed from persecution it became popular and rich and many pagans came pushing in. What was their belief about God? Many people think that pagans only believe in idols or in such Gods as we read of in Greek history but this is not so. They do believe in an absolute deity who is far away, and self sufficient, but who is so far away as to be unknowable to man. The gods whom they worship are the intermediaries between that far distant god and men and are fallible and semi-human with human passions and desires like men.

When St. Paul went to Athens he found amongst many altars one to " The Unknown God " (Acts 17. 22-31), that is to the absolute being, far distant from the world, unknowable to men. St. Paul preached the Catholic faith, the faith in wholeness, to them. " He whom ye ignorantly worship declare I unto you. God that made the world and all things therein, seeing that He is Lord of Heaven and earth dwelleth not in temples—giveth to all, life and breath and all things, and hath made of one blood all nations of men that they might feel after Him and find Him, though He be not far from every one of us, for in Him we live and move and have our being—for we are also His offspring." Now, it was this pagan idea of God which was brought into the Church in the fourth and fifth centuries and which gradually displaced the faith of St. Paul and what was taught by Jesus. This apostasy became the faith of the Church which then came to believe that a Vice-Regent or Pope was needed on earth as the intermediary between men and the God who was far away up in Heaven. The whole Medieval system developed on this basis.

What was the result?

1. Rome became a World State, the Kingdom of God on earth, " Civitas Dei." There was no need to seek the Kingdom of God, it had come and was the Church of Rome. The purpose of the Church was to save souls into this ark of salvation. The world was a " Vale of

tears " out of which the Church must rescue souls for Heaven.

2. The whole purpose of the Kingdom, the purpose of God to incarnate Himself in all creation and the sacramental nature of creation was lost sight of.

3. The Church's system of authority changed. It became an authority imposed from above; autocratic, totalitarian, a dictatorship, in spite of our Lord's warning, " it shall not be so " (Luke 22. 26).

4. The sense of God's immanence was lost and the Church ceased to be the Body of the Risen ascended Christ, working and redeeming and healing. It became more concerned to offer services of worship to the Christ above.

5. The Holy Ghost became identified with grace which was ministered through the clergy by means of sacraments.

6. The sacraments ceased to be the high lights of a sacramental creation, an intensification of the sacramental nature of all creation and the means of restoring man and creation to its true nature and then became rites performed by the Clergy and unrelated to life.

7. God became separated from creation, and religion from life, and this has led to a complete neglect of any sense of mission or of world redemption or of the social Gospel and it has led to an extreme pietism of the Billy Graham type and of many of the " Bible Christians " who centre all their religion on personal and individualistic piety.

Today we are witnessing a growing revolt against this paganising of the Catholic Faith. A theology which thinks of God as entirely transcendent is quite as heretical as one which thinks only of Him as immanent. The truth is that God is transcendent — that is He is greater than His whole creation. He is " high and lifted up " and perfect in all His being. He is " the Holy one that inhabiteth eternity " but also by the creative activity of His eternal word or

Son, the second Person of the Blessed Trinity, and by the grace of His Holy Spirit, the immanence of His transcendence is in all the world: He is its light and its life (St. John 1. 1-11). Matter is the vehicle, or sacrament, of spirit and there is a unity and a wholeness of all in God.

As a result of this recovered faith we are coming to a deeper consciousness of the indwelling of the Holy Spirit and of the unity of all things in God, to a true Catholicism.

We are becoming more aware of our own relationship to Christ as members of His Body — the Church — and therefore of our unity and responsibility with and towards all other members and of His Ministry and Healing through His Body, the Church.

We are seeing the need for study of our Lord's teaching about the Kingdom of God and gaining a greater sense of responsibility for the condition of the world and of people of all nations.

God has become real. Christ is with us now, and we are called into fellowship with Him in His purposes for the world: and the Christian religion ceases to be an escape from the world and becomes its only hope of salvation.

## CHAPTER IX

### MAN'S NATURE

It ought to be clear to those who have followed me thus far, that the healing ministry of the Church is the ministry of Christ through His Body, the Church. God is at work in every blade of grass, in every cell of our bodies: "The earth is the Lord's and all that is in it" (Psalm 24. 1). And God is adequate to our needs: "The Lord is my Shepherd, therefore can I lack nothing" (Psalm 23. 1). Can we believe that this is literally true? There is no magic method or technique of healing. Any methods that we may use must aim at bringing the sick person to a personal encounter with Jesus Himself, for He is the only Healer. And so it is not a matter of finding "a Healer" with a gift of healing or a Priest to administer the sacraments. What the person needs is to find Christ, the Leader to the Kingdom who ever works to overcome the evil which lies behind all dis-ease and all disease. When we know Him truly we can let go of all self-concern and fear, even of death and suffering; and experience the peace of God. This complete surrender brings not only peace, but a deep sense of God's love and fills our hearts with calmness and joy. We have found the pearl of great price (Matthew 13. 45-56); and the Holy Spirit has taken possession of our souls and is able to re-integrate soul and mind and body with the Spirit of God and begins to make us whole.

Now there are various methods by which this can be brought about: some of them very simple. By preaching the Kingdom of God; by the sacramental ministry of the Church, the laying on of hands, anointing with oil, or the Holy Communion: by strong suggestion or by the physical ministry of medical science: and in all these methods and many others God is at work. He is not tied to his own appointed methods, and the fact that someone is healed is no proof that the method which was used to help him is the only method, or even that it will be the right method to be used for the next person to be helped. "Except a man be born anew he cannot see the Kingdom of God" (John 3. 3). It is when the Holy Spirit takes of the things of Christ and shows them unto us, that we see the Kingdom of God at work and the Kingdom of God comes near to us in healing. So, also, "the Spirit bloweth where it listeth" (John 3. 8). The Ministry of healing is not by methods of our devising. It is the work of God.

But there is a ministry and there are methods and there is need for understanding, not only of God and how He works, but of man and how his nature acts. We say that our human nature consists of soul and mind and body, but these are not three water-tight compartments, they inter-act upon one another and are a unity.

*Mind affects the body;* we see this in the way that angry thoughts will cause the heart to beat fast by a rise in blood pressure; we become "hot under the collar" and have a flushed face as well as angry looks. *The body can also affect the mind.* Serious physical illness will incapacitate a person's mind. Mental illness of a very severe kind can also be caused by poisons from a physical focus of disease in the body reaching the cells of the brain.

*The body also affects the soul.* The spiritual deadness and depression which follow influenza or jaundice has been experienced by many and after an operation, the shock may deprive a person, for a time, of all spiritual perception. *The soul also affects the body*: the emotions of resentment, anxiety and worry, fear and many others, cause, under certain conditions, what are called psychosomatic diseases, which are often very physical.

And, of course, *the soul* or the spiritual life *affects the body* in a positive way and shines out in a person's face and character, which reminds us that man has spirit as well as soul and mind and body, and that these are a unity and must never be treated in complete isolation from one another. Man is a spiritual being and he needs to be whole or at least to be making progress towards wholeness: wholeness will be full likeness to God and only Christ Himself could attain to it, but in Christ and with His grace we are made to grow like Him and to glorify God not only in our souls but in mind and body as well. But only " When I wake up after His likeness shall I be satisfied with it " (Psalm 17. 16). It is through the teaching of psychology that we have learned a great deal about man's nature and most of all about the way in which his mind works. This knowledge still waits for its full significance to be applied in the development of man's spiritual life and to the healing of much mental as well as physical disease.

## CHAPTER X

### SPIRIT, SOUL, MIND, BODY

" I pray your whole spirit, soul and body may be preserved blameless unto the coming of our Lord Jesus Christ."

So St. Paul speaks in 1 Thessalonians 5. 23. As a trinity in man's make-up, that is good enough: for mind, which also comes in, can be looked upon as a function, partly of the body through the brain, and partly of the soul through the unconscious mind: mind providing the intelligence of the whole person. Every cell in the body has a minute unconscious mind, which is linked up with all other cells, giving the intelligence which enables each cell to function as needed in any part of the body; so that cells continue to form bone where needed and hair where needed, so there is no chaos in the body. Mind is not all in the brain.

Mind has three levels or differing functions, which are closely related to one another. 1. *The conscious mind* is that with which we think at any moment and normally we can only think of one thing at a time. That is why the toast burns if, for a moment, our mind is taken off the toast while we think of something else. 2. *The subconscious mind,* just below consciousness, has memory which holds many events which we may want to think about some day: There is now in your sub-conscious mind at this moment some memory which you can easily recall. What were you doing yesterday afternoon, or last Christmas Day? You can recall these and many other memories, as you will, from the sub-conscious mind. 3. But there is a deeper part of the mind than these: *the un-conscious mind,* in which is stored memories, which, normally you can't call to consciousness: memory of everything you have experienced since birth and possibly before that. And attached to the memory of events is all the emotion or feeling which you experienced at that time, so that the memory of some event early in your life which frightened you, will still be there with all the fear attached to it. We also have a tendency all through our life to repress or push down, into this deep part of the mind any unpleasant or unhappy experience, but though, as a result, it is out of sight and memory, it is still in mind. Now the emotion attached to memories buried in the unconscious mind is always trying to push up into consciousness: not the memory of the event, but the feelings connected with it:

and often it is able to do so in disguised forms in dreams, which is what makes some dreams so fantastic, but also important. It is also this emotion which pushes up into the conscious mind and causes the misery of a nervous breakdown: For we all need and use nervous energy with which to keep unwanted emotions down. It is on these three levels of our mind that we need discipline and healing if we are to grow into wholeness.

Now we must define our terms. Spirit is the creative life of God within us: what St. John speaks of as " that light which lightens every man coming into the world " (John 1. 9), William Law speaks of it as a seed of Divine Life within us which has all the riches of eternity in it and is always wanting to come forth into expression. Isaiah has the same belief about Israel: " My servant art thou in whom my glory shall break out " (Isaiah 49. 3). Spirit is the creative substance of our whole being, that which with God's grace enables us to grow into true sonship to God. It is what makes our human nature akin to God's nature; and if soul and mind and body respond to it and become deeply conscious of it, enables us to bring forth the fruits of the spirit.

*The Body* is the outer form which the creative life of God within us has enabled us to build into our means of self-expresion in this life. It has gathered water and chemicals from the earth and built them into expression of what we are in soul and mind and character. We drop off this outer form when we go on into the next life, for we shall need a new body then: and again the creative life within us will build the resurrection body suited to the conditions of that life. " As the days of a tree are the days of my people . . . for they are the seed of the blessed of the Lord and their offspring with them " (Isaiah 65. 22-23). A tree grows and develops and brings forth fruit and then comes to the end of its span of life and before going on into the next span of life it drops off its leaves, for it will need them no longer. But the tree goes on into the winter and begins to prepare to take on the glory of the spring. What a parable of life!

*The Soul* is what we speak of as " I." We say, " I think this," or " I will do that." " I am alive now but my body will die and I will still be alive." It is the whole human personality which expresses itself through the body, but is not permanently tied to the material world. " Unto Thee, O Lord, I will lift up my soul " (Psalm 25. 1). These differing functions of the one person are never isolated from one another. They interact upon one another and are capable, through a deep knowledge of God, of becoming the means of God's own self-expression and of experiencing His eternal life. " For this is Life Eternal that they should know Thee the only true God and Him whom Thou didst send, even Jesus Christ " (John 17. 3).

As the thoughts and feelings which fill the deepest part of our minds, our unconscious minds, are always expressing themselves in our characters and in our bodies, it is very obvious that a deep knowledge of God and of His love and joy and peace and goodness will gradually express itself in us and through us and enable us to grow into His likeness. This is what God desires for us.


## CHAPTER XI

### BODY SOUL RELATIONSHIPS

A human being is a unity of spirit, soul, mind and body and disease is a dis-function in this unity. Wherever the disease or dis-function may be, it affects the whole person. It is the person who is ill. The trouble may begin in our environment, either in our physical or our mental environment. It may begin in body, soul or mind, but the whole person is involved.

We are not, as people used to think, the helpless victims of invasion by germs or outside forces, so much as, quite often the victims of ignorance or of infections from other peoples' thoughts and minds. The human race is a unity and there is contact with other peoples' minds on a deep level, so that we are susceptible to what others are thinking around us. A disease may be largely due to some sustained emotional condition and yet there may be several contributory causes, wrong feeding, bad sanitation, bad economic conditions, bad housing, a shock, or even very negative ways of thinking. The accumulated effects of these may be what we call racial evil or heredity: and much illness comes in this way. When children are born with defects of mind or body it is seldom the fault of the parents. This kind of defect often skips a generation and is due to dis-ease several generations back. It is in the healing of the whole social order that the healing of such ills will come. A cleaner race will produce healthier children. And God's redemption through Christ must deal with all the evil of the race. It is the work of the Church to promote this. The whole creation " groaneth and travaileth in pain with us " (Romans 8. 19-22), waiting for its redemption which must follow ours.

As far back as 1920 I read of experiments which were being made at Harvard University, in U.S.A., in which they discovered that the chemicals in our blood vary according to changes in the emotions being experienced in the mind. They even claimed that by applying litmus paper to the forehead they could tell what emotions were uppermost in the person's mind at the time. From these early beginnings have grown a whole new approach to disease. Psychosomatic medicine today realises the need of dealing with the deep sustained emotions, if physical cure is to be achieved. Every emotion which passes through our souls has its effect upon our internal ductless glands and in a minute way pours chemicals into our blood stream or affects the internal secretions of the body, or in some cases affects the balance of the hormones in the body. Thus a feeling of shame quickly brings a blush, fear makes us tremble, the thought of food makes our mouth water, sorrow brings tears, joy laughter. In each case the stimulus has been thought which leads to deep feeling. All this is our every day experience about which we are not deeply concerned. But excessive emotion of harmful kinds can cause disease and we know that certain, if not all, negative emotions, if continued with frequently, can cause serious illness. Thus skin diseases, duodenal and gastric ulcers and rheumatism and rheumatoid arthritis, indigestion, boils, headaches, and many other illnesses, as well as many pains which seem to have no physical cause, are due to negative emotions; such as anger, hatred, jealousy, fear, anxiety, worry, resentment, bitterness, deep sorrow and grieving and frustration, in other words, stress and strain.

This would be very depressing if we didn't also know that positive emotions such as love, joy, peace, happiness, contentment, success, confidence and faith all have the opposite effect, because they also affect the internal glands in our bodies, but pour health-giving and stimulating secretions into our blood stream and affect the body for good. In a normal person who is well and living a balanced life emotions of various kinds pass through the mind and are not very lasting and the good and bad effects cancel one another out. But through no fault of their own someone may have conditions in their lives which are very difficult and day by day a feeling of frustration and bitterness grows and is a daily and hourly feeling for months or years. As a result, harmful chemicals begin to saturate the blood stream and the body which is always getting rid of poisons through the breath and urine and sweat, cannot deal with the quantity now accumulating. The result is disease, which continues until the emotional condition is changed. A very deep grief caused by the loss of someone we love may mistakenly be repressed, so that no tears flow, and the matter is not spoken of to anyone. "What marvellous courage," we say: but such emotion will certainly find an outlet and often does so in asthma or bronchitis or in some other form, sometimes in severe physical pain in some part of the body. There is much still to learn and room for research in this whole field and those who have to help sick people can learn much from the large numbers of books on psychosomatic conditions. It seems as if there is an organ language in which the body betrays the inner workings of the mind, but woe betide the would-be helper of the sick who relies upon his observations too rigidly. Medical science tries to deal with these conditions through psychiatry and by more and more drugs, and we must welcome every relief which can be given in these ways, but the deep dis-ease, the emotional condition, must be met by spiritual means and it can be reached and changed by deep meditation in which the positive knowledge of God changes what is negative and therefore stops the flow of poison to the body. Where these conditions exist, and they do so very frequently, it is part of the ministry of the Church through her ministers, to deal with them. It is debasing to the ministry of the sacraments, for instance, to anoint a person suffering in this way and to expect healing when we have failed to use the knowledge which is now available to us for removing the cause of the disease. The healing of, shall we say, deep resentment through a deeper experience of God's love is the ministry of the Church which brings salvation, rather than other methods which might be used. We must be very elastic in our ministry and suit our methods to peoples' needs.

* Someone will ask, what about accidents? And of course they do happen, but many are due to emotional causes. It is said that 85% of the accidents which happen, do so to 15% of the population. A large number of people are accident-prone as a result of emotional instability. Records have been kept in large factories where thousands of workers are employed, and if all those who have accidents are taken off the out-door staff and put into the factory, and others are brought out to fill their places, the only difference has been that while the accident rate goes down for the out-door staff, the rate rises inside the factory for the same people continue to have accidents in their work inside the factory.

And germs? Yes, they are always with us and many of them are very helpful in many ways, but even germs which cause disease are often in our noses and throats and do no harm, and are unable to harm us unless we give them the conditions in which they can multiply. This we do largely, by allowing our emotional life to become negative and thus making the blood stream toxic.

# CHAPTER XII

## WHOLENESS

God's purpose for us as individuals is wholeness, a wholeness which reflects his own character and life. That is clear from all our Lord's teaching about the Kingdom of God. Wherever His will is done and His Kingdom comes, all evil is overcome and His own perfect life is expressed. It is obvious that we will none of us attain to this fully in this life, but we must aim at it. And so it is never enough for us to centre our thoughts and hopes and efforts on becoming just physically well. God is himself "the Holy One." "As He that hath called you is holy, so be ye holy in all manner of conversation; because it is written, Be ye holy; for I am holy" (1 Peter 1. 15), and God's holiness includes a completeness which is perfection, which He intends to express in His whole creation and therefore in us. Therefore it is no surprise that Christ, who was God in the flesh, healed the sick and sent His Church to heal, and told people that, far from disease being God's will, it is always His will to give salvation which means health.* When Jesus spoke of eternal or everlasting life He used the Greek word " aionios " which means much more than life after death. It is life which has all the quality and strength and power of God's life. It would better be translated overmastering life. It is God's purpose that we shall experience this kind of life and not

---

* " St. Paul's thorn " does not indicate that it is God's will that sickness should continue: nor that God sent the thorn. St. Paul wrote about his weaknesses in II Corinthians 11. 18-30, and they are all connected with his persecution; there is no mention of sickness. It is the weaknesses caused by persecution in which he says he will glory (Ch. 12. 5). The thorn in the flesh (12. 7) is a messenger of Satan, not God's will. While St. Paul suffered this weakness he knew that God's grace would be sufficient for him, but nowhere is it stated that God would not heal him. And meanwhile, he says, he will take pleasure in his weaknesses " in injuries, in necessities, in persecutions " and so on (12. 9-10). If St. Paul had thought that God sent sickness and willed it, would he ever have healed anyone?

death, which Jesus said those who live in ignorance of God are living in now (John 5. 24). A Christian is a person who has experience of this life and knows its power in his life. He has passed " from death into life." The tragedy is that we are not conspicuous for it. Instead of being people who manifest the joy and the love and the peace of God and His wholeness and health we are often no different from those who don't know God at all. We are often depressed and we worry and get anxious and resentful and are easily offended and unkindly critical of others and as a result these dis-eases of the soul express themselves in our bodies in illness and disease : we have colds and headaches and nervous breakdowns like anyone else. These things ought not to be. We can be and we ought to be whole, expressing God's wholeness within us. But we can only achieve this through a very deep knowledge of God which enters into the deep unconscious mind and heals our consciousness. We need to learn to live from the centre instead of from the circumference. Unless we are taught how to control ourselves we tend to draw our feelings — that is our emotional life — from the things we see and hear, the cinema, wireless, television, from advertisements on the hoardings or from what we see and read in the papers or from cheap novels. Do you realise what an immense amount of garbage, of sin and evil comes in, deep, into your mind from the world around every day? And that this is all having its effect on your whole character and body? How like limpets we are. They squat on the rocks and wait to feed on all the garbage that passes by on the tide. But we are not limpets : we can choose what we feed our minds with. As we think, so we become. The mind builds what is deep in our mind into expression in our bodies, often in disease. People sometimes ask, when they are seriously ill, " Why has this been sent to me?" In their suffering they think of God, and with wrong ideas in their minds, blame Him who never sends sickness and never punishes but overcomes suffering and evil by suffering it with us as He did upon the Cross. Oughtn't we to ask ourselves more often, what thoughts of evil, what negative thoughts have I allowed to fill my mind that this has come to me? It may not always be possible to see the answer, but the power of evil in the world is very great and much illness comes from it, though we may be entirely blameless: but there is not one of us who is not involved in it, because it is all around us. And yet we can learn to live from the centre and it is the work of the Christian Church to teach us how to do so.

God is always within us as well as around us. Jesus said, "Lo, I am with you always," and that means now. And where Jesus is, there is all the power of God (Matthew 28. 18-20): and that power and strength is in you always. That is the centre of your life as St. Paul knew: "I live, yet not I, but Christ liveth in me" (Galatians 2. 20). He lived from the centre. "I can do all things through Christ which strengtheneth me" (Philippians 4. 13). Unfortunately, very few Christians learn to live from the centre. Their whole religious life is far too much on the surface. They say prayers and they go to Church, but they very seldom sit still and let God speak to them and make Himself known to them. The result is that very little of the knowledge of God and of His goodness and purity and love and peace sinks into their souls and into their deep unconscious minds. The result is that there is far more of the evil of the world and of the wrong values of the world buried in their minds than knowledge of God, and evil predominates and leaves us little different from those who are not Christians.

Now this need not be. We can learn to live from the centre and come to know in our own experience that God is real and always within us and that His strength and goodness can be ours. We do this in meditation, and particularly in a very simple kind of meditation which goes very deep. But before we go on to think of this we must think of the life of prayer, out of which meditation springs in the natural growth of our union and fellowship with God.

# CHAPTER XIII
## PRAYER

There have been great changes in thought and understanding during the last sixty years, not only in science and psychology but in religion, and these have brought a great need for a change in our ways of praying. Sixty years ago *science* was mechanistic; scientists thought that creation was inevitably moving forward under the leadership of science to a perfect state of society; there was no need for God or religion. Matter was thought to be solid and indestructable. This has all changed. No scientist believes this today and there is a far greater humility in scientific thought. Whereas sixty years ago hardly any scientists were Christians, today there are many.

Sixty years ago *psychology* was a new play thing and rather a joke to most people: but it has won its way and it has taught us to understand the way in which our minds work and the immense importance of the unconscious mind to both medicine and religion.

Sixty years ago *medical science* was dealing with the body, specialising on separate organs, entirely materialistic in it's approach. Today psychosomatic medicine has emphasised the importance of the mind and the emotions and medical science is coming to see that it is the person who needs to be healed and not only the body or the mind. It needs still to realise the vital influence of spirit on soul and body.

And again, sixty years ago we talked about the clergy as " sky pilots " and of " going to kingdom-come." God was, for most people, in the sky, and we believed that the purpose of Church-going and of " being good " was that we might go to heaven when we died. Charles Kingsley's jibe was deserved, religion was " pie in the sky when you die." Today we are only slowly beginning to believe again what our Lord and St. Paul taught. " I am in my Father and ye in me and I in you " (John 14. 20): that God is " the Father of all who is over all and through all and in

45

you all " (Ephesians 4. 6): that God, as well as being the Creator and greater than all, is in the world, filling both heaven and earth (Jeremiah 23. 24): and that He is concerned to bring His Kingdom on earth as in heaven: and that the purpose of religion is to enroll us as His helpers in this purpose.

Yet, in spite of all these great changes, many people are still tied to prayers and hymns which speak to God as if He were far away above the clouds, and as if the only purpose of the Christian life was to get us to heaven. There is great need for thought and change in our methods of prayer. Prayer does not call to a god who is far away, nor do we have to hammer at the gates of heaven as if God was asleep; we do not have to sway God to our own purposes and persuade Him to do what we want. Balaam is spoken of as the man having his eyes open (Numbers 24. 3): so is the man of prayer. Prayer is the attitude of one who is aware of God all around him and in him and in all men and at work, always for the good of all creation. God is no stranger to His own universe, breaking into it to perform wonders or to pay it a short visit. He is in all things and nothing in the world exists apart from Him or without His knowledge and care and purpose. God never changes. He is the same yesterday, today, and for ever, and prayer doesn't change Him. It can change those we pray for.

Prayer then, is first, understanding, knowing that God is real. " Be still and know that I am God " (Psalm 46. 10), but also knowing the good news which Jesus brought, that God's purpose is to overcome the evil of the world and to bring His Kingdom into being and that we are called to work with Him for that purpose. As soon as we realise this fully we will become conscious of the real state of the world and of our own involvement in it's evil and how unworthy we are to have union and fellowship with Him. The more we know through Christ's teaching and character, of the goodness and love of God, the more we will feel this unworthiness. This leads to penitence; we know our sins and our unworthiness and we confess them and seek God's forgiveness which is always waiting for us. Confession is not the act of a weakling, but of one who knows his need and desires closer fellowship with God: he wants to disassociate himself from the evil which is separating him from God and making him unfit to serve, or to receive God's gifts.

Then, although our first steps in prayer will probably have been selfish and self-concerned, asking for this and that which we wanted, we begin to be more concerned in prayer about God's purposes than our own. So, our Lord gave us the Lord's Prayer as a method of prayer, in which there are seven petitions, but none are selfish. It is a method of prayer. Jesus said, "after this manner pray ye" (Matthew 6. 9). We begin with personal relationships. The word "our" includes other people and we ought to stop and think who we mean by "our." We may mean just our own family, but we can also make it a prayer which goes out to include all mankind, or someone who is in special need. Then we go on to pray each sentence of the prayer for those we have in mind, as well as for ourselves. The one we pray to is Our Father in Heaven: infinitely great, creator of all, who is perfect love and goodness, in whom is no darkness (1 John 1. 5). And because so few people believe this we pray "Hallowed be Thy Name," that is, that God may be known truly as He really is, so that those for whom we pray may be able to honour Him. How can anyone honour God unless they know Him truly? So we go on to pray for His purposes for the world, "Thy Kingdom come, Thy will be done on earth as it is in heaven," for that is what we desire above all things, not only for the world but for each one we pray for, whatever their need. Then "give us this day our daily bread" and no more than our share of all the good things of life. Forgive us our sins as we forgive those who sin against us, which means that if we don't forgive we ask not to be forgiven! How we need to learn to say all this sincerely. And "lead us, not into temptation" because unless God does lead us day by day, we shall certainly go astray in a world such as it is today.

"But deliver us from evil." The evil which besets us on all sides and has even now got its grip upon us so that we know that we are infected by it. And then all comes back to the real purpose before us. "For thine is the Kingdom, the power, and the glory for ever." This is the best method of petitionary prayer; and one which we can use, saying it slowly and thoughtfully every day, including in it the names of friends and relatives and the needs of the world.

NOTE: for fuller teaching on prayer read my "*Growth in Prayer.*" 2/6d. James Clarke.

## CHAPTER XIV

### MEDITATION

There are several methods of meditation and most people are taught, at some time, about one of them. The most common is "*discursive meditation.*" In this method you take a passage of scripture and read it carefully and try to picture the scene and think about it, trying to learn from it. You allow the subject of it to stir your feelings, it may be of love or penitence, and you end with prayer and resolutions. All this is good training and a valuable form of Bible study as well. By using it regularly people learn a great deal more about God and it should lead them on to the expression of their love and devotion to God. Many people, however, make this such a great intellectual effort that they don't get beyond knowing more about God and they need a method by which they can learn how really to know God Himself, in their own deep experience. Most people need a further method of meditation which will take the knowledge of God deeply into the unconscious mind, where, as we have seen, so much worldliness and negative thought lies and where emotions attached to buried memories are waiting to be redeemed and healed by the grace of God. We all need a great change of consciousness on the deepest level of the mind.

This is done by the method of *" contemplative meditation,"* which is a step in the growth of our prayer life between meditation and contemplation: it is, what is often called " affective prayer," or the prayer of affection.

This method is based on our belief that the Holy Spirit is always within us; and in Him is all that is in God. " Ye know Him for He abideth with you, and shall be in you " (John 14. 17). " Son thou art ever with me and all that I have is thine " (Luke 15. 31). So also St. Paul speaks of God as the Father " Who is over all, and through all, and in all " (Ephesians 4. 5). We aim at learning to know this truth of God's indwelling love and joy and peace and strength intuitively, so that we can rely upon Him in our daily life. So, we sit, best of all in a straight backed chair, in a disciplined way; both feet on the ground, back straight, head up, hands on the lap and eyes closed. In this way we can be entirely relaxed as well as disciplined, and we begin by relaxing and getting quiet in God's presence. Then we take a simple sentence like " My peace I give unto you " and repeat it, in the mind, over and over for — to begin with — three or four minutes. We don't try to think about it or what it means, we relax, not only the body, but also the conscious mind, and let the truth in the words sink into the deep unconscious mind. The repetition of the sentence helps us to hold the conscious mind in quietness and helps to prevent it thinking and wandering.

The sentence needs to be carefully chosen; and it is better to use one provided in a book on the subject than to choose one at random oneself. It must be centred on God: " Be still and know My peace within you: " or " Be still and know that I am infinite love within you: " or " I will bring you out of darkness into light." We use the words " infinite " or " eternal " because that distinguishes its quality from its earthly equivalent. The peace of the world, for instance, is the peace of escape, escape from war or escape from toil: the peace which comes when the children have gone to school, whereas God's peace is deeper and gives a calmness in the midst of stress. We don't try to think this out during the meditation, we allow the truth to sink, relying on the Holy Spirit within us to lead us into full understanding and truth. It is a real waiting on God; not expecting to hear with our ears but knowing that God is real and that he does speak to the soul or to the unconscious mind.

This method of meditation ought to be a regular part of our prayer life every day. We decide beforehand how long we intend to meditate and then keep to it by a watch or clock however difficult it may be at first to continue. We don't expect any sort of uplift or feelings, even of peace, while we are doing it, because the effect of it is on the deepest part of the mind and soul which is unconscious. Yet there will be results. As we persevere our deep unconscious mind becomes healed of its deeply buried emotions and then there is a gradual build-up of positive truth — God's peace and love and joy. Then we suddenly realise that we are becoming calmer in our whole approach to life: we do what we have to do without worry or anxiety and don't fuss about the next thing we have to do, because the peace of God has grown in our souls. We may find that we are meeting difficult situations more constructively, our personal relationships have become easier because the love of God is expressing itself in our daily contacts. This, and a deepening sense of joy, are the proofs of the practical value of this method, not what we feel at the time of meditation.

Someone will say, " but is this not just suggestion?" No, it is something more than suggestion, though we will not be frightened by the word " suggestion," which only describes the way in which our minds are working every day. It is not the kind of suggestion taught by Coué, when you try to get the mind to accept something which is not true but which you want to be true. It is the quality of a suggestion which is important, and in the case of meditation the sentence expresses the Truth and God is Truth. But we are not sending this Truth down into a vacuum either, because deep within us is the Holy Spirit and what we send down calls out what is already there into expression. We have capacities for the expression of all the qualities of God's life and character within us, and meditation by this method calls those qualities forth into our lives. " My servant art Thou in whom My glory shall break out " (Isaiah 49. 3).

This is what I think St. Paul meant when he said, " Be ye transformed by the renewing of your mind " (Romans 12. 2), or, " Have this mind in you which was also in Christ Jesus " (Philippians 2. 5).

## CHAPTER XV

## HELPING OTHERS

The thought of the wholeness, as well as the holiness, of God leads us to a belief in the wholeness of creation as God's purpose : and man who is made in the likeness of God is made to be whole. The nature of the Church also derives from God : and wholeness ought to be one of its marks. There is a unity of spirit amongst its members : we are one body " and whether one member suffereth, all the members suffer with it " (1 Corinthians 12. 26). Some people believe that there is a unity of consciousness in the human race. It is strange how new thought arises at the same time in far distant places in the world. Whether this is true or not, it is quite certain that mind touches mind on a deep level of consciousness, and distance seems to be no hindrance. People call it " telepathy." It is certainly true that one person can spread panic or depression and that children very quickly sense unhappiness in a home and become uneasy and insecure. But there is something even deeper for those who are members of the Body of Christ. There is a unity of spirit and a deep sharing of consciousness within the Body which is Christ in the world.

A person who is ill, either physically or mentally, is in great need of awareness of God and of a knowledge of His love and peace and of the perfect goodness and wholeness which he is always working to express in every one of us. Therefore, knowing our unity with the sick person in God, we can meditate for him. We take a meditation just as if we were meditating alone. " Be still and take hold of my peace within you:" We go on quietly meditating, repeating the sentence for a little time and then we bring the person's name into mind, not in any way trying to push the words into his mind, but certain that on the deepest level of the mind he shares in the truth that fills our deep mind. The deeper our own consciousness of God and of His peace becomes, the more the sick person will be able to draw from us for his need. Don't, whatever you do, try to use your will. It is not you who can heal, only God can do that. But the consciousness of God's peace in your mind will help to disperse the stress and strain in the sick person's mind.

Some years ago I was sent for to help a young man who had been waiting for an operation for ulcerative colitis. He had developed very quickly septicaemia, an embolism, and then pneumonia. The doctor thought he was dying and he was unconscious. I had seen him often and he had a deep faith in God. First, I talked to his mother and helped her to put him into God's hands and trust Him for life or for death. Then I sat and meditated by his bedside. He was quite unconscious. The words I used were, " I thank Thee, Lord, that Thy will for him and for me is wholeness, healing and peace." I was completely silent all the time. Two hours later he opened his eyes and began to recover. He told me a few days later that his first thought on recovering consciousness was of the wondeful peace he felt and he knew before he went to sleep that night that all was well and that he was going to get better. There was no magic in that healing. God is the only healer and He does not work by miracles. This young man had caught the faith which he needed for God to heal him from my deep mind and the peace and the love of God in his heart had brought reintegration of soul and mind and body. He recovered and went away to convalesce. This method of meditation can be used to help people who are mentally ill. I discovered this when I was

Chaplain of a mental hospital for five years. With many mental patients, their conscious mind is very confused and has relinquished all control and they are under the control of sub-conscious impulses. It is as if the real person is standing back and watching. Their sub-conscious and unconscious mind is very open to influence. That is why the atmosphere of a mental hospital is the largest factor in healing. This means that by meditation you can reach their deep minds and give them an awareness of God's love and joy and peace. There are, of course, hindrances to this — a deep antagonism to religion embedded in the mind or surrounding scepticism amongst the nurses or others can completely nullify our efforts, but apart from this, those we meditate for will catch the sense of God's love or peace and use it as a sort of sill or ledge to hold on to, by which they can pull themselves up, out of the abyss that they are in. No patient's mind or soul is a vacuum. Christ is within, and Christ is within us and that is the point of contact on the deepest level, through meditation. When we are helping people who are ill we must learn to think and feel positively about them: that is, we must know that God is at work in them and that He always works to heal and to give life. There are always two things to remember about every situation however distressing. There are the facts and there is the truth. So we look at the facts: it may be the person has cancer and is not expected to recover, or the person is mentally ill and the doctor's prognosis is very distressing. We must put these facts into God's hands and surrender them. Then we look at the Truth: God is at work, he is adequate to the situation; He is always good; His life is now in the person. " I will never leave you nor foresake you, trust in me and be at peace."

Outer conditions are not the most important thing. The disease is often the outer expression or symptom of a deeper dis-ease. It is the inner consciousness which is important: circumstances can and do change as it changes. Of the Christ, Isaiah says (Isaiah 11. 3 and 4), " He shall not judge after the sight of His eyes, neither decide after the hearing of His ears, but with righteousness shall He judge," so we must see people as God has made them to be, not dwelling on the evil they have fallen into, but on God.

So often in Church after some bidding to prayer people are expected to respond to " O Lord, hear our prayer," by saying, " and let our cry come unto Thee." It would be much more positive to say, " Father we thank Thee that Thou hast heard us," with the response, " Therefore, we give thanks unto Thee for ever." We have much to do to bring the prayer life of the Church into line with our deeper knowledge of God and to make our prayers effective for God's purposes. We so often pray and receive no answer, " because we ask amiss."


## CHAPTER XVI

## MEDITATION AS A THERAPUTIC METHOD

There is always a cause for sickness and disease and it is always the whole person who is ill, not just one of his organs. In Chaper XI we saw the way in which soul and mind and body interact upon one another, and how the deep emotions affect mind and body. So true is this that we can almost say that there is a body language. It is not always easy to read it and unless you are very careful you may be led widely astray: but stiff and hardened limbs often betoken some stiffness or hardness in character: blindness sometimes comes from a refusal to see something important: deafness can be from a refusal to listen: a blush expresses shame and a white face fear. Symptoms do give us a clue to a person's real and deep need, but let it be only a clue which leads you to further seeking of true causes. Only experience in helping people who are ill will give you the intuition needed to know the kind of emotional disturbance which is, through the action of the internal ductless glands, causing the physical symptom.

I have found in my own experience, which now runs

into nearly 50 years, that in cases of rheumatoid arthritis there is always an emotional condition causing the toxic condition of the blood stream and so the inflammation in the cartilages in the joints and thus the pain. This emotional condition is nearly always unknown to the sick person. It is a deeply buried bitterness and may have arisen in early childhood, as a result of some frustration causing bitterness. But it may be due to some conditions in later life — the loss of someone upon whom the person was dependant, or a change of living conditions which are not congenial. It is very rarely anything blameable because it is so often due to some memory, with emotion attached, in the deep unconscious mind. It is quite possible for this condition to be healed if the person who is ill understands what is happening and is prepared to co-operate. The remedy is persevering meditation by which the knowledge of God's love and forgivingness and peace is dropped into the deep unconscious mind and very gradually changes the deep consciousness. At first it dissolves the bitterness and then begins to build up a positive content in the deep mind in its place. It is necessary for the person to meditate several times a day and even in between the set times to have a sentence in mind which can be repeated in the train or bus or while washing up or doing chores. I have never known complete healing to take place in less than five months of this persevering practice, and in some cases it takes longer, but I am confident that it is a real way to healing and as it is also building up a deeper knowledge of God, it is the way towards greater wholeness. I have known children who have been healed in this way and a woman of seventy-nine who lost all her pain and was given exercises to loosen her limbs and became quite mobile. This does not mean that joints which have become distorted by the disease are healed, but that the emotional condition is changed and therefore the poisoning of the blood stream ceases and the inflammation dies down and therefore the pain ceases. There is often a great increase in the pain for a week or two before it ceases altogether. This is due,

I think, to the fact that the meditation is reaching down to the depths of the mind, to the deepest layers of negative feeling, and changing it. People have often told me that the pain was getting worse and was almost intolerable, and all I have been able to say was, " Go on, even more frequently, with the meditation," and then, quite soon, the pain has gone for ever.

Now an interesting thing about all this is that there is no need to try to find a memory of bitterness. In most cases it is entirely hidden in the unconscious mind and the person is unable to remember anything about it. But in some cases, after some weeks of meditation, there will be an abreaction, that is, the feeling of bitterness or resentment or whatever it is, comes up into the conscious mind during the meditation. It may also bring a sudden recollection of what caused it, but not always. If this happens, the person must know how to deal with it. He must ask himself, " Where does this feeling come from? It certainly comes from my deep unconscious mind and is a feeling connected with something earlier in my life. But there is no need for me to go on feeling it." So he starts to meditate to dissolve it; saying, " I forgive; I forgive; I want to forgive as you forgive, dear Lord." Saying it slowly and using it for meditation for a week. This will dissolve the bitterness and be a large stride towards the ultimate healing. During the whole of this spiritual treatment, the person will be advised to continue any treatment being given by medical science. The right kind of medicine can help to change the metabolism of the body, and to counteract the toxins. The medical treatments ease the symptoms : but the meditation deals with the deep cause of the trouble by bringing the knowledge of God's love and forgiveness and peace deep into the soul, where His salvation becomes effective.

This process of meditation and the abreaction which it brings about is a very important factor in healing. It happens very frequently when it is used to help a person with any neurotic trouble. The symptoms may be that of a nervous breakdown, or of some deeply buried complex, or fear or hatred. The person has no idea of what is buried in the deep mind from childhood: but with persevering meditation the buried complex and even memories quite forgotten tend to come up into the mind without the disturbance of deep analysis. They can then be faced and understood and dissolved by further meditation. This leaves the person much more integrated and more positive in thinking, and with a sense of confidence in God. I have found that some people who have been sent to me by psychiatrists, or who have not responded to psychiatric treatment — deep analysis and electric shock treatment — have responded to spiritual treatment and have recovered. Not in every case, however, does an abreaction occur: I think probably only with those in whom the emotional condition is very strong and deeply repressed. In many others the meditation deals with the emotional condition which causes disease by bringing about a change of consciousness on a very deep level of the mind and soul. In this way the emotional stress and strain which causes so much physical illness can be dealt with and healing then follows, and as it is accompanied by a deeper knowledge of God and a more Christian way of life, the healing is to the glory of God and fulfils His purpose for the person who has been ill, in making him more whole. I fully realise that this is a method which can only be used by convinced Christians, but we are considering the Christian Ministry of Healing and our work is to bring people to faith in God.

## CHAPTER XVII

### PREPARATION FOR THE HEALING MINISTRY

*First* of all, the person who is to minister to others must prepare himself. This is far more important than any preparation which the sick person may need. The Minister must be certain of the reality of God and know that he has authority to speak for Him. He must be God-conscious and so be entirely unself-conscious. He must know the real presence of the living Christ within himself, as well as within the person he ministers to, for that is his point of contact with the patient. In my own experience nothing but regular day to day meditation will cleanse the deep mind of scepticism and fear and self-consciousness, and deepen a consciousness of Christ within. It deepens our intuition into the needs of others and our awareness of Christ at work, redeeming and healing: and of His calmness and peace and caring love. We can train ourselves to walk with Christ through the streets on the way to the sick person's house, and to walk upstairs behind Him and to know that He bends over the sick person in compassion with us. And " in-as-much as ye did it to one of the least of these, ye did it unto me: " the sick person is part of the body of Christ and it is Christ's own life in His body which heals. In fact, the healing ministry is Christ at work through us and in us and a service done to Christ Himself in the sick person.

*Secondly*: you must be a good listener. Don't rush in with your own teaching and talking. Encourage them to talk. Almost all illness has an underlying cause and it is mostly emotional stress and strain, which is often quite unknown to the patient. It will often reveal itself to an understanding listener in the way in which the sick person behaves. Hesitation in speaking about something often precedes an outburst of penitence. Tears often precede the pouring out of grief which has been repressed for a long time. Don't interrupt with sympathy or with questions, let the emotion come out into the light. Eighty per cent. of those who are ill need to be able to talk out their problems before they can see the way through: and it is far better they should see the way through themselves than that you should tell them the way. If you have enabled someone to do this by being a silent listener for an hour while they talked and cried, you will have done more for them than by giving advice. If the person hesitates and is silent, you must pray to the Holy Spirit in the silence. If they stop and say, " I don't think I can tell you," just say,

" Well, let us be quiet for a short while and ask the Holy Spirit to help us."

Never, under any circumstances, show surprise or alarm or impatience, or condemnation, or blame, and never be shocked by what you hear. We are helping people in an interview, not judging them. Some people find it difficult to get out what they want to confess. There may be an excessive feeling of guilt about some sexual event or habit which, when it comes out, is often of little importance, and about which there need be no feelings of guilt. If real sins are revealed and confessed with sorrow and desire for amendment, absolution should be given at the end of the interview, without expecting the person to go into Church and to confess it all again in a formal way.

*Thirdly*: we ought to be learning from all that we hear and see, how to help them, if they need it. As they pour out their feelings and their problems, you may be able to see what particular emotional stress has been poisoning their bloodstream, causing the physical illness or pain from which they are suffering. Don't point it out to them. Help them to find it themselves. All the time you are learning how much their religion has been real in their lives or not; how much you will have to teach them; what wrong ideas will have to be corrected; how far, in some cases, they may have been finding their illness a way of escape from some impossible situation; whether they are " enjoying ill-health " for any reason; whether they want to get better and whether better physical health is all that they want. As you watch the person's face, you will see when there is something which they fear to speak of, something that makes them self-conscious, something which makes them tense or bitter, and you may have to encourage them to get it out and to see it clearly.

All this is preparatory to the teaching which you will need to give. If the person has revealed any underlying emotional condition, you will have to help them to understand how this has had its effect on mind or body and you will need to teach them how to change this deep emotion and how to replace it by the deep knowledge of

God's love or forgiveness or peace. This can only be done by teaching and by deep meditation. You will have to win their co-operation and help them to see that there is no magic or quick way to healing.

What I have written applies largely to people who know their need of help. They are ill and they may have tried every other method of being healed: they may have been to doctors and " healers " and now they have heard that you can help. You may have to make it clear that you are not " a healer " and have no power to work miracles: only God can heal and He needs our co-operation and faith in Him, not faith in being physically healed and well. God has made us to reflect His own wholeness, and we must seek it, for only a deeper wholeness which comes through Christ's power can lead us to the perfect fulness of life which God wills for us.

A Priest or Minister working in a parish will come across sick people who have no idea of all this. They may only expect him to make a social call and to talk about the weather. They may only want to talk about their symptoms and may have no expectation of being healed. They may even resent the idea that there is any cause for their illness within them. He will then have to begin where they are and explain the way in which the mind works, the power of evil in the world, and how we are involved in it; the unconcious influences which have affected us; and he may possibly have to give a great deal of simple teaching before he can hope to bring such a person to the point of ministration. But all this is the work of healing. Every person is different and some are more responsive than others. A Minister doing sick visiting regularly week by week will do well to have a course of teaching ready in his mind for some weeks ahead and to keep a small book in which he can keep a record of the stage of teaching which was reached with the person at the last visit, so that he can continue it at his next visit. He would then make his visits purposeful. People would soon learn to look forward to a short Bible reading, a short instruction, and a period of silent meditation which could be continued and used every day till he was visited again.

* Children have sometimes to be helped. A child with a stammer or a physical disability or it may be with a disease. It is very important to begin by making friends. It will help a lot if you have an interesting watch to be looked at or if you can make a paper model. Try to get the child to sit beside you on a couch, so that you don't talk at him or her; let him talk and if possible let off tension. In this way you will lead him up to the point of being able to help him to a deeper awareness of our Lord. Children can be taught to meditate and often love it, for it makes religion real and deep.

But most of the help needed for the child who is ill must come from the parents' minds. Any anxiety, stress or fear in their minds will certainly be conveyed to the child's mind, causing a sense of insecurity, and will be a hindrance to healing. If the parents can be helped to surrender their self-centredness and anxiety, a load will be taken off the child's mind: and if they can learn to know God's peace the child will be helped enormously. In dealing with diseases like polio and leukaemia which produce distressing symptoms very quickly, I have known quite as quick changes for the better when the parents have been quickly co-operative and have surrendered their child to God's care and known His peace deeply in their own minds. Children are affected very quickly by the atmosphere of the home, and are aware of disharmony between parents before they actually hear any angry words. A happy home makes happy children and healthy children as well.

## CHAPTER XVIII

### TEACHING A SICK PERSON

Jesus " sent forth His disciples to preach the Kingdom of God and to heal the sick " (Luke 9. 2). We must do both. Our Lord's teaching about the Kingdom of God was teaching about God and about His purpose for men and for creation. Our Lord was Himself revealing God. " I am in the Father and the Father in Me " (St. John 14. 11). I and My Father are one. " The Son can do nothing of Himself but what He seeth the Father doing " (John 5. 19). God is obviously at work in the world and Christ was working with Him and God's life had been at work in the world from the beginning. " He was in the world and the world was made by Him and the world knew Him not " (John 1. 10). This is the first truth which we must get home to people's hearts and minds: God is with us and in us always; and is always at work, wanting to be known and trusted, as He enables us to grow into His likeness as true sons and daughters reflecting and expressing His own life and character. So we point people, as Jesus did, to God working in nature, in the grass and seeds and flowers, and then point out how much more He is at work in us. God works on the natural level and we trust Him, because He never fails — for instance, in the harvest. How much more ought we to be able to trust Him as He works on the deeper spiritual level. And those who trust Him do come to know that He never fails. The whole creation is a great process of incarnation. Life is all the time and in every stage of creating expressing iself more and more fully. Often much hindered in expressing the perfection of God, by evil and lack of response, but always pressing on to overcome evil and to incarnate God's perfection.

When Christ came into this incarnational world, He did incarnate God, and those who knew Him best recognised His perfection. He Himself said, " I and the Father are one " (John 10. 30), and St. John speaks of Him as " the eternal life which was with the Father and was manifested unto us " (1 John 1. 2).

We believe that God is working in all creation with the ultimate purpose of expressing His own life fully and completely in the whole creation, and that this will then be His Kingdom on earth as in Heaven. So when Christ came to earth " that eternal life " of God which He manifested, was God on earth in all His power. It was that " Eternal Life " in Christ which healed the sick, raised the dead, stilled the storm, multiplied the loaves and fishes, for nothing is impossible to that life. " All power hath been given unto me in heaven and on earth." The Life of the Kingdom of God was on earth in Christ. It was in Him and He tried to teach men to know, that by faith in Him, its power is available to us. We are, in Christ,

" inheritors of the Kingdom of Heaven " * and its powers are available to us by faith. It is this faith in God which we need to recover, not faith that we will be healed physically, which is only self-centred faith, nor faith in any healer with power in his hands, but faith in God : and that is in one whose plans and purposes are not confined to this life or this world, but whose purposes will be fulfilled in His Kingdom. This was the faith of St. Peter when he said, " Thou art the Christ, the Son of the living God," and Jesus answered and said, " Blessed art thou, Simon . . . for flesh and blood hath not revealed it unto thee, but My Father which is in heaven " (Matthew 16. 16, 17). If we can bring a sick person to this simple faith in God, then he will be able to get the attitude to his sickness which Isaiah attributed to the Christ in Isaiah 11. 3-4: " He shall not judge after the sight of his eyes, neither decide (R.V. Margin) after the hearing of his ears, but with righteousness shall he judge." That is, he will not centre his mind on the symptoms of illness, which may be serious: nor will he centre his mind on what the doctor says or people are thinking, and again the prognosis may be hopeless: He will judge with " Righteousness," that is, he will know God's perfect will and purpose of wholeness. God has made this person to express His own wholeness and God's life is in him working for it. This is the attitude of faith, both for the person who is ill, and for all who love him and surround him. This is the point of view of one who believes the Gospel of the Kingdom. And as mind touches mind this is the attitude of faith which will help the sick person. Any negative thought in the minds of people around him will hinder his recovery.

If someone who is very ill can be brought to this simple attitude of faith, he will be able to face the circumstances

* Our Lord speaks of " the Kingdom of God " and sometimes of " the Kingdom of Heaven." These both mean the same thing. The Jews didn't like to use the name God, which was too holy for common use. So the word heaven was used sometimes instead. Compare the parable of the Prodigal Son. " I have sinned against heaven and in thy sight " (Luke 15. 18).

as they are: the fact that he has, shall we say, a cancer, or disseminated sclerosis, so often spoken of as " incurable : " the possibility that he may be going to die very shortly : the probability that there will be much pain : the possible parting from loved ones. These are the facts, but they are not the whole picture : for God is with us now and He is at work and He understands and is reliable. We can put the facts into God's care and lose our self-pity and self-concern, our fear. If death comes it has no fears, for God is real and His purpose for us is not death but life, and His purposes go on for ever. So there comes to the Christian soul the moment of complete surrender to God and the experience of His peace in the knowledge of His love. This brings an intense sense of joy and trust. He has found salvation in Christ: the Holy Spirit has taken possession of his soul and mind and reintegrates his whole being with the Spirit of God within.[*]

In my ministry to sick people, it has been this experience of peace and surrender that has again and again been the moment when recovery has begun. It is certainly the moment for the Church to minister its sacraments, for individual faith is not enough. We are members of the Body of Christ and the Church is that Body and is the instrument which Christ has formed for His own use. A Sacrament is " an outward and visible sign of an inward and spiritual grace given unto us, ordained by Christ Himself, as a means whereby we receive the same and a pledge

[*] *Fasting.* Our Lord speaks of fasting in Matthew 6. 17-19. In Mark 9. 29 and Matthew 17. 21 He is answering the disciples' question, " Why could not we cast it out?" saying " This kind can come out by nothing save by prayer and fasting." In Acts 14. 23 we see that the Early Church used fasting with prayer. There is no doubt whatever that the mind can concentrate more deeply when the body is at rest, and that it is easier to sustain prayer and devotion for longer periods when the body is not busy with its digestive processes. When we have cases of serious illness which we are praying for and little progress seems to be made. it often helps if a small number of people will give a morning or three hours to concentrated prayer and meditation, taking nothing more than a cup of tea on waking till after the period of prayer. My experience has been that quite often this marks the turning point towards recovery.

to assure us thereof " (Catechism). So our preparation of the person who is ill must be supported by the life and faith and understanding of the Church. In so much of our ministry to the sick at present it is this faith that is entirely lacking.

In all this preparation of the sick person's outlook and faith, we will encourage him to accept all the help and advice which he can get from medical science, which is also one of the channels through which God works. God uses penicillin as well as prayer, and some people need much more physical help than others. It is no more a sign of lack of faith to accept this physical help than to receive our daily food, for God has made the world and all that is in it for His own purposes and has put into it a supply for all man's needs. So we receive God's gifts with thanksgiving both for soul and body. Christ brought a Corporate Salvation into the world and we shall be saved as members of His Body, deriving help from many members. We are none of us just individuals.

## CHAPTER XIX

## VISITING AND HELPING SICK PEOPLE IN THEIR HOMES

In a parish it is very necessary that the Vicar or Minister should give regular teaching to the congregation about the healing ministry. In this way they will learn to know that their Vicar or Minister is able to help them when they are ill; and then they are more likely to send for him or ask him to help them in time of trouble. They will also begin to realise how much their own prayers can help those who are sick and they will want to meet with others to support their Vicar's ministry.

The Vicar, and some lay people who have been trained by him, will visit those who are ill, in their homes. It is essential that their attitude to sickness should be right and that they should go to people who are ill with intent to help them to a deeper wholeness of soul and mind and body, and that their thought of them should be entirely positive. Disease is always a symptom, it is not an entity in itself, and so we are concerned to bring healing to the deep cause, whatever it may be: it may be sin, or stress, or strain, or some deficiency of emotion. The function of the body is to express the condition of the soul and mind and so we need not be too concerned about the physical aspect of the illness. The doctor will be doing his best to help physically and we must remember that some cases need more physical help than others. So, the less we talk or think about the symptoms, the better. God is at work and He does all things well and we can trust Him, and the more certain we are of that, the more quickly will we convey that certainty to the person we are visiting. If you can't be positive in this way, you would be better on your knees waiting on God to give you faith; because we so quickly convey our own attitude of faith, or lack of faith, to the people we visit, and if we are negative in thought, we may actually hinder a person's progress instead of helping them.

You will see, then, how important it is that those who visit should be people who are prepared for their work, and this will be done best by regular daily meditation, bringing us to a deeper knowledge of God's life and power always within us. It makes all the difference in the world to our ministry if we pray daily for those who are sick, and if we wait on God for the intuition and wisdom which enables us to become aware of their individual need, and perhaps of what is either causing their illness or hindering their recovery. Prayer and meditation of this kind helps us to grow in grace and in faith in God: and what we *are* always helps people far more than anything that we say to them. As our faith grows, we think less of people as " chronics," or " incurables," and far more of God at work within them and of His purpose of wholeness, which won't always be attained in this span of life " because of our unbelief," but will be attained in the triumph of His Kingdom. We must learn to be good listeners: let people talk and never interrupt. Let them talk out their problems and don't solve them for them. If you do this, they will see their way through. And if the person stops talking, don't talk yourself, train yourself to be silent and to pray and to know the presence of our Lord. If something crops up which is difficult, or if the person can't get out something which is a trouble — just say, "Let's be quiet for a few moments and ask God for His help." If you do this, the person may be able to go on and get out something that will help you to a deeper understanding. Don't ever condemn and never show any surprise: here is someone who is trusting you in their need and their deepest need is to know Christ through you. When the moment comes for prayer, don't pray at length. You will find that it will help to use silence after short biddings. "Let's be quiet now and seek a deeper knowledge of God. Give us knowledge, dear Lord, knowledge of Thyself" (silence of one minute). "Now try to say these words over and over in your mind, ' Be still and take hold of my peace within you ' (silence one minute). Then, "Thank you God." People learn to pray if you give them silences and it sinks in deeper — " said " prayers pass over peoples' heads.

You must be careful in visiting people who are very ill not to stay too long, or you tire them and make them worse. If you find someone full of fear, try to get them to accept it as something which will surely come to them again and perhaps again, but to know that if they will let God come into their hearts and minds every time with the fear, His perfect love will change and cast out the fear. Get them to say over and over several times a day, " Thou art in My keeping and in Me there is nothing to fear," or just, " fear not, for I am with you."

Death is a terror to many people and we ought to give much teaching about it. Death does not separate us from God. If we have been members of Christ's Body — the Church — on earth, we ought to look forward to being still a member of His Body after death, and of growing in grace that we may come to the place prepared for us in His Body, to being part of " the full grown man." If death is faced and prepared for by repentance, there need be no fear of it, and simple trust and peace will take the place of fear.

You will also come across people who look on themselves as " chronics " and are quite hopeless of any recovery or even improvement. " You see," they say, " this is incurable," or " the doctor says," and they are quite faithless and hopeless. You must be very persevering in not allowing them to be negative about themselves. Try to get them to put the condition which they are in into God's hands, knowing that His will is their wholeness, even if it does not come in their life-time on earth. I can remember a man who had been bed-ridden for 40 years, paralysed from his waist downwards: he was also blind. I knew his doctor very well. He started having what appeared to be trances. He would become quite rigid for several hours. In one of these he got out of bed and walked round the room. A friend who was with him told him about this and persuaded him to try to walk and found that he could do so, and for many years he walked quite a lot. People become obsessed with the impossibility of recovery — we must not. We must not judge after the sight of our eyes: nor after the hearing of our ears, but see people as God has made them to be (Isaiah 11. 3), and hold this truth in our minds and prayers.

Unbelief in the minds of doctors, nurses, and often of many Christians, surrounds people whom we try to help, and it is the biggest hindrance to God's work. Jesus was so certain that God's will was to perfect the whole creation as His Kingdom and that nothing was impossible to Him. The only failures were due to the unbelief of those around. " Why could we not cast him out," asked the disciples. The reply was, " because of your unbelief " (Matthew 17. 19). And in Nazareth, " He could do no mighty work there because of their unbelief " (Matthew 13. 58). We pray for people and their condition may change, but if in their deep unconscious mind there is the conviction — " I can't get better," they are not able to take advantage of the improvement. You must teach them to take the T off the word can't, and say, " I can do all things through Christ."

And then remember that as you go to visit the sick, you do not go as an isolated individual, you are a member of Christ's Body and so is the sick person. Remind him of this and of his unity with the Body and of the prayers being offered for him and give him a sense of his unity with them in Christ. It is we who are sick in them for we are all one in Christ. It is Christ who needs their healing for His Body's sake.


## CHAPTER XX

### THE LAYING ON OF HANDS

It was our Lord's practice to lay hands on the sick (Luke 4. 40). " When the sun was setting all they that had any sick with divers diseases brought them unto Him and He laid His hands on every one of them and healed them." In Luke 13. 13, " He laid His hands " on the woman who had a spirit of infirmity for eighteen years and healed her. In Matthew 19. 15, He laid His hands on small children. In Mark 5. 23, Jairus asks Him to come and lay His hands on his daughter for her healing. In Mark 6. 5, " He could there do no mighty work, save that He laid His hands upon a few sick folk and healed them." And then in Mark 16. 18, the laying of hands followed by healing is one of the signs which will follow on belief in Him. In Acts 28. 8, St. Paul laid his hands on Publius' father and healed him.

In the Early Church the ministry to the sick was exercised by the laity using oil blessed by the Bishop or Presbyter and by the laying on of hands : and prayers were provided in the earliest service forms (liturgies) for this purpose. For fuller historic details on this subject the leader is advised to read in " Liturgy and Worship " the detailed article on " Visitation of the Sick " by Charles Harris (S.P.C.K.).

The laying on of hands is given in two different ways. " A healer," that is, someone who claims to possess a natural gift of healing (see Chapter 22) will place his hands on the part of the body which is affected by disease. He will often pass his hands down the person's spine or almost forcibly unlock the locked limbs, sometimes using such strength that he needs the help of an assistant " healer." Some " healers " are capable manipulators and physiotherapists. They are using power which is their own. Quite distinct and different from this is the minister, priest, or authorised lay person who gives the laying on of hands as a Sacramental act. He will lay his hands on the head of the sick person, after careful preparation (see Chapter 18). He has no thought of anything physical passing from himself to the person who is ill, in the use of a Sacramental Act.

The Catechism asks the question, " What meanest thou by this word ' Sacrament '?" And answers, " I mean an outward and visible sign of an inward and spiritual grace given unto us, ordained by Christ Himself, as a means whereby we receive the same and a pledge to assure us thereof." The laying on of hands is all this.

1. The laying on of hands is the " outward and visible sign of an inward and spiritual grace given unto us." The grace given to us is the presence within our souls of the love and joy and peace of God's Holy Spirit which comes into action the moment we have real faith in God, as we cease to be self-centred and become God-centred.

2. The laying on of hands was ordained by Christ Himself for he used it and he sent His disciples out to preach the Kingdom of God and to heal, and they would naturally do as He had done.

3. It is the " means whereby we receive the same and a pledge to assure us thereof." The laying on of hands is given usually by a priest and his ministry is that of

the Church which is the Body of Christ. Therefore, it is Christ acting through His Body who lays His hands on the sick person: just as it is Christ acting through His Body who breaks the bread in communion. What the person receives is Christ's healing and this sacramental act assures the sick person of this.

The Minister would, therefore, do well if he were to wait for a few moments after placing his hands on the person's head in order to realise, that his hands are the hands of Christ's Body, that with Him and in Him are all faithful people bringing the healing and redeeming power of Christ to bear on a sick member of the body — the Church -- which is their own body. "If there is a thorn in the foot the whole body must stoop down to pull it out." "We are His flesh and His bones" (Ephesians 5. 31 A.V.). There is real contact between member and member within the body and the life of the Head fills every member. If, in the teaching given to the sick person, all this is explained, the laying on of hands comes to him with great assurance. A woman once wrote to me: "You gave me the laying on of hands nearly two years ago. I knew then that something had begun in me. Now I am completely well. The recovery has been slow but sure."

This ministry ought to be given frequently in Church, either after the offertory at a Parish Communion or at the end of a Service before the blessing: but only to people who have been prepared or who know how to prepare themselves. But the congregation in such cases must also be instructed and know how to pray positively for wholeness and not merely for physical betterment, or else they will hinder the healing by their wrong thinking. People take the ministry of the doctor for granted; they see his car outside a house and they know what he is doing; they will only take the Ministry of Healing for granted and lose their expectation of magic, when they see the Sacramental Act being ministered to people who may not be in danger of death but for whom they are being asked to pray. If the sick person is unable to come to Church the ministry should be given at the time of ordinary sick visiting. As a rule " the laying on of hands " should be given by a priest or minister. It is true that the whole Church is a priestly body. But for Holy Order's sake certain people are commissioned to act in certain ways for the whole body. If there is no priest available for baptism or for the laying-on of hands, then a lay person will be right to exercise the office. And, of course, lay people are often commissioned to use this ministry.

When the ministry is given in Church it is always good to have one or two lay people assisting the priest in the laying-on of hands to emphasise the fact that Christ is healing through His Body, the Church, It is also natural for a Christian mother to lay hands on her child as she prays for him when he is ill. What is strongly to be avoided is that lay people should be claiming the power to heal as individuals going about as " healers " leading people to expect nothing more than a little betterment of the physical body, such people draw attention to themselves rather than to Christ. It is always important to remember that Jesus Himself was not " a healer." He healed by the power of that Eternal Life which was in Him: it was the Life of the Kingdom of God in Him. All His works of healing were " signs " of that Life being present: they were " the mighty works " done by the power of that Life. So with us, self must stand back: the living Christ is the only giver of Life and wholeness, and He is one with the Father and the Holy Spirit.


## CHAPTER XXI

### HEALING SERVICES

While I think it is good that people should be ministered to, by the laying on of hands or by Holy Unction, in the Church where the other members of Christ's Body can show their care for the sick members, by praying for them and assisting in the ministration: I do not think that healing services should be held to which anyone can come without preparation. People often say, "But Jesus healed all who came and didn't prepare people at all. Why all this fuss over preparation?" But Jesus did prepare people. In spite of the fact that the Jews were a religious race with a very real background of faith, which people in our Churches have not got today, He was continually teaching people about the Kingdom of God. This teaching is almost entirely lacking in the teaching of the Church today and has been lacking for hundreds of years. Yet it was the Gospel — the good news of God's purpose — and our Lord taught people to see that his works of healing were done by the power of the life of the Kingdom in Him: they were not miracles but "signs." "If I by the finger of God cast out demons, then is the Kingdom of God come upon you" (Luke 11. 20). And besides this, Jesus "knew what was in man" (John 2. 25) and we don't. If He saw the cause of illness, He could deal with it at once. "Son, thy sins be forgiven thee" came before "take up thy bed and walk" (Matthew 9. 6): "Go, and sin no more lest a worse thing come to thee" (John 5. 14).

I have taken many healing services in the past. In some Churches I have taken healing services at intervals for years and I noticed several things.

1. That the same people come over and over again. They had not been healed, although I am sure they derived a certain amount of uplift from the service; their expectation of healing must, I think, have grown less. I can't think that this helps to make the ministry effective.

2. I have generally asked people to give thanks for healing if it comes and that they should let me know. But I have had very few cases in which this has happened as a result of healing services. On the other hand, I have a very long list of names of people who have written to give thanks after their recovery when they had been helped and prepared and shown how they

could seek for Christ's healing through faith and prayer.

3. I think that any centring of expectation on physical healing is a hindrance to a person being made whole. Self-centredness is a condition of sin and our aim must be to centre a person's thoughts on God, at work, within. Healing services lead people to expect physical healing and sometimes physical healing alone.

4. The people in the Church look for magic. I have seen people standing on the seats at the back of a Church, to get a better view and being disappointed that nothing sensational was happening. These people often go away with wrong ideas in their minds —"Either God can't heal or He won't," as someone said to me. However careful the Minister may be in pointing to God as the only healer, people do tend to think of the Minister as a "Healer."

5. Many people come to healing services expecting that they will be healed, who are suffering from diseases which need a great deal of understanding and very careful treatment through prayer and meditation. A case of rheumatoid arthritis can be healed by persevering meditation which gradually changes the deep emotional condition which has caused it, but not by ministry at a healing service. And so it is with many other diseases which have a deep emotional cause. There is no magic in Christian healing and while many people claim that they are "healers" and that they are able to do miracles of physical healing, it would be well to read (Matthew 24. 24; and 7. 22), and to ponder on it (also see Chapter 22).

Why did the Church lose its Ministry of Healing in the early centuries? (see Chapter 8). There were, of course, great changes in Christian thought at that time: but there was also a great concentration on physical healing and on the use of "healers," people with charismatic gifts. In fact the possession of such gifts was looked on as a sure sign that a man had a vocation to the priesthood. By the

74

fourth century Christians were taking sick people to the shrines of the saints who had healed in the past, and seeking healing by relics. The whole ministry had fallen into superstition. Is the way back to the recovery of the Healing Ministry in the Church by a return to these methods?

I can't help believing that the Church is the Body of Christ and that it is through the life of the Church, through its love and fellowship and prayers and faith that Christ heals today. The Holy Communion is the service of healing at which people should be ministered to if possible. There the bread of life is given to preserve both body and soul unto the everlasting life, that is to fullness of life within the fellowship of the Church. I fully realise the sincerity of many people who conduct healing services and I have no doubt whatever that people find them much more interesting than many of the ordinary services of the Church, but this is not the purpose of the ministry of healing. And I believe that we will only postpone the full recovery of the ministry as a normal part of the activity of Christ through His Body by continuing to use these methods. The way forward is to make the Church as it gathers for Communion a real body, a community in which all the members really care for each and each cares for all: a Body which is a real fellowship, which misses the absent sick member and prays for him or her with real faith and visits them. A body to which the outcast and the patient discharged from the mental hospital will want to come, because he knows that he will find love and caring and a welcome and people who know the presence and the peace of the living Christ. A Body of Christ like this would begin to see Christ's healing going on before their eyes; they would become a healing power in the world attracting others to its healing and to the salvation or health which Christ came to bring.

It would be in a healing Church and as part of the healing Body of Christ that people who had special gifts would join. I would like to see in every large parish a gathering of Church members each week to which handicapped people would come, crippled and lame, blind and ill people, those with nervous breakdowns, ex-mental hospital patients: in fact any who are suffering from the stress and strain of life and with them members of the Church who have learned to live vitally and to think positively and are men and women of prayer, who really care for others. They would meet in an atmosphere of prayer and much teaching. They would divide up into groups for painting and pottery and rug-making and other interests, giving one another an interest in life. There would be teachers and doctors and physiotherapists and an osteopath and any who had gifts of healing or of artistry or any other gifts of the spirit, bringing them into the service of Christ in their fellow men — none of them known as " healers " but all contributing by their various gifts to the Ministry of Christ through His Body — the Church — to a deeper wholeness by the giving and receiving of His love. In this we would have the Healing Ministry in action. St. Paul speaks of these varied gifts of the Spirit active in Christ's Body, the Church (1 Corinthians 12), and in the last verse of that chapter says, " And now a more excellent way show I unto you." He then goes on in 1 Corinthians 13, to speak of the way of love in which all these gifts meet in the love of God. Here, in all this activity of friendliness and caring, would the living Christ be at work healing through His Body, the Church.

## CHAPTER XXII

### " HEALERS "

We often hear people being spoken of as " healers." The word is applied sometimes to sincere Christians who have and use a healing gift. But the same word is used of those who promote and advertise large healing meetings and do their healing with much publicity. This has become a money making business. There are also " healers " who charge large fees for the laying on of hands and for advice. They, most of them, lead people to expect " signs and wonders " in the way of physical healing. This way of working degrades and hinders the Church's Ministry of Healing and frightens people and puts them off thinking about it seriously. We must try to see what is going on and see the element of truth which lies behind it.

And first of all we must realise that a great many people have a natural gift of healing. Some have it much more strongly than others. This gift is sometimes used quite naturally by doctors and physiotherapists and nurses without their being called " healers." St. Paul reminds us that members of the Body of Christ have various gifts (1 Corinthians 12. 4-15; and Romans 12. 4-21), prophecy, healing, teaching, psychic, and so on, but they are all gifts of the one Body which is Christ at work. He is the only Healer and uses all the varying gifts of the members of His Body. What is wrong in people who claim to be " healers " is that they are acting as if they were the whole Body. " But the body is not one member but many " (see 1 Corinthians 12 to end).

Some people have a healing gift much more strongly than others. It can be felt: their hands become very hot: with others there is great vibration. These " gifts of heal- ing " have been known for thousands of years. " Healers " worked in the pagan temples both in Greece and in Rome, and they were known to our Lord. Sick people were taken to the pagan temples and put to bed there for treatment. This gift is probably related to the gift of " dowsing " or " water divining," which many people have, or even to such a simple thing as " green fingers." We all have radiation in our bodies and some people seem to have it nearer the surface and so become aware of it, in the same way that some people have psychic gifts, while most people are not aware of them. Gifts of this kind ought not to be exploited; they can be used wrongly and become a danger; they have their use as we shall see later.

Psychic gifts are often exploited in spiritualism, which not only leads people astray from the Christian religion and gives wrong teaching about life after death, but also seriously endangers some peoples' mental health. Psychic gifts will be of great value to us after death but are not needed in this life. A very large part of the manifestations claimed by spiritualists are explainable by psychology and by an understanding of the way in which our minds work. If a person is psychic he can easily read what is in your mind, and we are easily deceived.

In the same way the gift of healing can be wrongly and even dangerously used. It is not always good to remove pain, which can be done by one who has this gift. Nor is it always good to heal physical symptoms without healing the deep emotional cause of the symptoms: it is often followed by a serious relapse. Our Lord said to the man at the Pool of Siloam, " Go and sin no more lest a worse thing come to thee " (John 5. 14). The cures which take place on the platform are sometimes very spectacular, but also, quite often, they are very short lived; for they are dealing with physical symptoms under strong emotional stress, and nothing spiritual is taking place, for these are gifts on the natural level. It is here perhaps that the greatest objection lies, because this kind of healing is entirely focussed on the physical healing and, therefore, on self, and even if the person is relieved of the physical ill, he is left in his self-centredness, which is a condition of sin. We are the children of God and His Life within us and can only become whole by becoming God centred.

Nevertheless, these gifts can help in the healing of some physical conditions, and they have their place, as we shall see in the Ministry of Christ through His Church. So now we must ask, what was *our Lord's attitude to " healers "* of this kind? He quite obviously warned His disciples against this concentration on the physical disease and healing. They were to be the salt of the earth, overcoming the corruption and evil which lies behind the symptoms. In His own healing works Jesus never used the word " miracle " in describing it, for there was no magic removal of what was unpleasant physically. His work was spoken of either as the mighty works (dunameis) done by the power of the life of God's Kingdom which was present in Him, or as signs (semeia) that the Kingdom of

God had come near or "come upon" them. His works of healing were not wonders (terata) and He warns His disciples of this "except ye see signs and wonders ye will not believe." Then He speaks directly of "healers" and warns His disciples that they are false prophets and false Christs doing signs and wonders and leading people astray (Matthew 24. 24). Then (in Matthew 7. 22), "Many will say to me in that day, Lord, Lord, did we not prophecy by Thy name and by Thy name cast out demons and by Thy name do many mighty works. And then will I profess unto them, I never knew you: depart from me ye that work iniquity." Why such condemnation? Surely God's purpose for us is wholeness; and wholeness can only be attained as we become God centred? And is it not wrong to lead people to seek and to be satisfied with anything less than this or with the self centredness which is sin?

But there is another quotation — (Mark 9. 38) — and this seems to contradict the above. St. John asks the question, "Master, we saw one casting out demons in Thy name and we forbade him because he followed not us." And Jesus said, "forbid him not, for there is no man which shall do a mighty work in My name and be able quickly to speak evil of Me, for he that is not against us is for us." At first sight this seems to cancel out what Jesus said about "healers" in St. Matthew, but we must note the context. At the moment when He was asked this question, Jesus was being hard-pressed by His enemies. His life was in danger. He had already been away to the borders of Tyre and Sidon to escape from the Pharisees (Mark 7. 24; and 8. 11). The Transfiguration has just taken place and Jesus warns His disciples of His coming death (Mark 8. 31). He wants to be quiet and is on His way to "beyond Jordan" (Mark 10. 1) to a place of retreat, before His coming ordeal. Now the disciples are making more enemies by forbidding "the healers" to use His name. How natural that He should say "Forbid him not — we have enough enemies already. He that is not against us is for us." And then following, Mark 9. 40, we have, I think, a short remnant of the teaching which followed his answer to the question. He speaks of His disciples being salt. Salt which deals with and overcomes corruption: for their ministry to the sick is to be no magic healing of the physical symptoms, but a real redemption and healing of the corruption which causes sickness. So he ends, " Salt is good. Have salt in yourselves and be at peace with one another " (Mark 9. 50).

There is no contradiction here but a strong corroboration. And yet, the Christians of the Early Church were to find a way of using these healing gifts of which we must speak in the next Chapter.


## CHAPTER XXIII

## A HEALING CHURCH

The last Chapter may have brought us to the point of being able to see what the Church's Ministry of Healing really is; even perhaps, to seeing more clearly what it means to be a Christian. God has made the world and the whole human race as part of it and there is a unity in it all. No single human being can live entirely to himself. Our very food comes out of the earth, we are part of it and we are dependent all the time on other people around us. Not one single human being in any part of the world who is suffering, is separate from the unity to which we belong; He suffers in us and we in Him. We cannot be whole till all is whole. This is what Christ meant when He said, " I am the Vine and ye are the branches:" and " Inasmuch as ye did it to one of the least of these, ye did it unto Me." God is in us, like your life is in your body and every soul in the world is of as much value to Him and loved by Him as, shall we say, your leg is loved by you.

Jesus formed the Church to be the beginning of making this a reality: it was to be a foretaste of His Kingdom, gathering the limbs and members of His Body together to learn to be a unity, a Body through which His love and caring, all for each and each for all, could work. St. Paul realised this and wrote of it in 1 Corinthians 12 and 13, and Ephesians 5. Do go back to these chapters and read them in a modern translation of the Bible.

St. Paul realised that every different member of the Church would have different gifts, enabling them to excel in some particular work. Some would be artistic, having the skill to paint or model or draw. Others could teach needlework or languages or history or music. Some would be able to preach or pray better than others. Some would be doctors, or psychologists or osteopaths or nurses or pharmacists. Others would have a gift of healing which could assist the healing properties in the body. Some would have greater, more simple faith, and others a deeper love and sympathy and understanding. One could go on enumerating every kind of skill and profession known in all the world. But all this skill and all these gifts and vocations are of God and by His Spirit and through His creative power, they can come from nowhere else. And the human race ought to be sharing in it all as a unity. So St. Paul reminds us that the Church is one Body and that all these gifts are the gifts and faculties of the life of Christ working through His Body, the Church. The artist needs the doctor and the doctor needs the baker and the baker needs the farmer, and we all need the love and the prayers of others, and we can't be whole without them. And so the various members of the body with their various gifts are the Body of Christ, through which Christ works to heal and to make whole and then to use for His purposes in the world. There is no idea of any one member being the sole source of healing. The love and the care and the human interest stirred by the teacher or the doctor or the linguist is quite as much used by Christ in healing, as the person who has a gift of healing. It is Christ working through them all who heals, and He is known to be the only Healer, and is glorified as such.

Have we not here the clue to real meaning of the Healing Ministry of the Church? And isn't the recovery of the true nature of the Church and a real expression of it in the *normal* life of the Church the way back to the recovery of it?

The usual way in which the Church sets out to help people who are sick or diseased, is by way of visiting them in their homes or by praying for them individually, generally at a distance, and thinking of them as " sick " and needing help, but in isolation from the body. They may receive the laying on of hands or be anointed with the Holy Oil, but it is unlikely that anyone will be there except the Priest. How far this is from what St. Paul speaks of: a Church which is a body in which all share in the sufferings of each and all are concerned; a body filled with the faith and power and life of the risen Christ bringing the life of His Kingdom into action; the sick member deriving and receiving all that he needs, in any way, for his healing from the wholeness of the whole body.

And doesn't our knowledge of the causes of sickness and disease help us to understand this, In most cases of illness there is either an emotional condition which is negative, such as resentment, bitterness, misery, fear: and each of these conditions is disturbing the metabolism of the body (see Chapter XI), but each of these is also a lack of something which the person needs. Resentment calls for forgiveness, bitterness for love, misery for sympathy and fear for assurance, and within the fellowship of the Church there are people who, if the fellowship is real and deep, are able to give of this spirit for the healing of the sick members of the Body. We are members one of another in a much more literal and true a way than we have yet learned to be. It is we members of the Body who seem to be so well, because we can be mobile and are lacking pain, who are really sick in those who are immobile at home through disease.

It is not enough to pray for individual sick people or the blind and deaf and crippled and diseased, they are part of the Body and we and they need one aother and need to pray together and to meet, not as people to whom we are doing good, but that we may learn from one another to know the Healing Christ who lives in us, and so to be healed of our loneliness and our resentments, and to be able to know the love of God as it touches us within the living Body of Christ.

To recover the Church's Ministry of Healing, we have got to break away from the idea of worship which sprang up after the fourth century, that of offering continual services of praise and prayer to the far distant God, as if that was all that the Church existed for. We must learn to be the Church by making it the gathering together of all the members sick and well, all bringing their gifts of teaching and wisdom and healing and above all love and caring, into the one activity of the living Christ, who alone can make us whole, because His Spirit is all that we need to enable us to become the manifestation of His incarnate life to the world in love, unity and integration.

## NOTES AND QUESTIONS

CHAPTER 23 NOTE

What should someone do who finds he is psychic or has a gift of natural healing?

1. If we have a psychic gift the best thing to do is to make real efforts to develop our prayer life and to learn contemplative meditation. In this way we will subordinate the gift to the work of the Holy Spirit and we shall find that it will increase our spiritual perception and intuition and make us more helpful to others and more powerful in prayer.

2. If we find that we have a healing gift we will do best to dedicate it to the service of God in the nursing or medical professions. In the use of our hands, in tending the sick we will find the natural outlet for our gift under medical supervision and for large numbers of people. Many physiotherapists and osteopaths are using their gifts in this way. Others may find a sufficient use for their gift in the occasional laying on of hands which will be given in a well developed life of the Church as described in Chapter XXIII. Not calling themselves "healers," but contributing to the expectation of wholeness by all members of the Church.

# CHAPTER XXIV

## HOW TO TAKE A PRAYER GROUP

It is quite possible for someone who is not in any way used to speaking to others about religion or to praying in public to lead a small group for Intercession. A group can begin with just two or three people and then gradually grow. From six to twelve people is a good size for a group. If it gets beyond sixteen, it may be wise to divide it and form two groups. A group may meet in a private house or in a vestry or in Church and lay leadership is good, for it trains lay people in leadership and responsibility. A group can spend 30 to 40 minutes in intercession and if desired it can then go on to discussion. It should never begin with discussion. A group will meet each week, or fortnightly, but preferably not less frequently than that.

Suppose that the time for starting is 8 p.m. people should be urged to come a few minutes early so that greetings can be concluded by 8 and a punctual start made. Don't wait for late people. The group will have a list of sick people for whom they pray. Some of these will be known to all, but others only to one person in the group. No name should be on the list of anyone who is entirely out of touch, at least with someone in the group, it may be only by correspondence. Each person to be prayed for must be in at least one person's mind, he is then in the group mind. The meeting of the group will begin punctually with the leader saying, " Now may we have reports," and he (or she) will read the list of names one by one, and anyone who knows the condition of the person will report — very shortly — with no mention of any details of disease or suffering. The leader will have to curb the desire on the part of some to elaborate details. At the end of the list other names can be added but there should be no compunction about taking off names of people who are better — with thanksgiving; and also removing the names of people of whom there are persistently no reports. If touch with them is renewed and they still need help, their names can be put on to the list again. A real effort should be made to keep the list short. Eight to twelve names are enough for any group. If the list grows longer, names should be grouped according to need.

It is to be hoped that as the love of the members of the group grows by intercession, so their interest in those they pray for will grow into real caring, which will lead to the visiting of the sick persons, and to enlisting the co-operation of those being prayed for by the group, by teaching them to be quiet and receptive at the time when the group meets, and helping them, by lending them literature on Christian healing, so that they become more positive in their faith and expectant of becoming more whole.

When the list has been read and reports given, which should not take more than five minutes, the leader will say, " Now let us be quiet and realise the presence of our Lord. ' Lo, I am with you always ' and that means now." Then at least two minutes of silence. Then can follow prayers and thoughts with spaces of silence, as given in " A form of intercession for prayer groups " (published by the Guild of Health, 26 Queen Anne Street, W.1.

In this way we realise the presence of God within us, and then we go on to realise our unity in Christ with all those for whom we are going to pray, and so their presence in Christ with us. Then the leader will say the name of each person on the list in turn, and after each name say a positive sentence of meditation.

Give me knowledge, knowledge of Thyself, dear Lord.
Trust in me and be at peace.
Be still and take hold of my strength within you.
I am never alone for Thou art ever within me.
I would be alive, dear Lord, with Thy life within me.
I am the light of health within you.
I thank Thee that Thy peace is ever within me.
I will bring you out of darkness into the light of health.

I will never leave you nor forsake you.

Fear not, for I am with you.

I will uphold and guide thee in all thy ways.

When you have said one of these sentences, the group will repeat it silently for half or a whole minute, and then the leader will say, " Let us bless the Lord," and the group answers, " Thanks be to God." If there are recoveries, thanks should be given, " Father we thank Thee that Thou has heard us."

" O Lord my God I cried unto Thee and Thou has healed me. Thanks be to God."

Then the group can go on to pray for all the world: for the Church in the parish, clergy, people who worship together, youth and children, etc.

For those who suffer — in hospitals, prisons, by persecution, hunger, war, hatred, etc.

For all who go to the far parts of the world for Christ, etc.

Then all is summed up in the Lord's Prayer together and the Grace.

In praying for children, always remember that children's deep unconscious minds are affected by the emotions in the mother's and father's minds. Therefore, pray for the parents that they may be able to trust God and unselfishly surrender the child to His care. If they can really trust in Him in this way it will help the child to get better. Children sense anxiety in their parents' minds, as they sense quarrelling, and are made to feel insecure, which is a hindrance to their healing.

In praying for old people there is no need to pray that they may die. God knows their needs far better than we do. Old people often have a lurking fear of death deep in their minds: so pray that they may know God more truly and be able to experience his love and peace. If they do this they will slip away peacefully when their time comes.

There will be no " chronic cases " to a prayer group with a real faith: their aim is not physical healing alone.

They will try to bring each person they pray for to such a simple faith in God that all fear and self concern will go and they will experience His love and peace. If that happens, they will begin to experience the life of God's Kingdom and to that life nothing is impossible.

There is nothing more thrilling than taking part in a prayer group which has really learned to enter into union and fellowship with Christ in His healing and redeeming work. If a list of people who have been prayed for and who have recovered is kept and thanksgiving is made for them now and then, the faith of those who pray will be strengthened as they give glory to God for His goodness.

## CHAPTER XXV

### INCARNATION

The great outstanding truth which the Christian Religion brought into the world was that GOD IS INCARNATE. What does that mean? It means that God is in the world and in all creation and in us: that He is working all the time to express His own life in everything that He has made. This does not mean that God is not also outside of everything. He is: He is greater than His whole creation and perfect in all His Eternal Being apart from it, but He is " the Father," not a carpenter; and He works in all and above all, to fulfil His purposes for creation. People speak of immanence and transcendence as if they were two different things. They are not. It is the immanence of God's transcendence which works in the world. There could not be any presence of God within all, if God were not all and in all, filling both heaven and earth. The incarnation of our Lord Jesus Christ as a Babe in Bethlehem was the great revelation of this truth. By coming into the flesh and living as man on earth, Jesus showed the truth that God has made our human nature to be the means of His own incarnation. And this makes it also clear that all creation is made for incarnation. The incarnation was not " a bolt from the blue," it was not a beneficent invasion, as if a God who has no relationship to His creation had come into the world and chosen to appear as man rather than as a great angel. No: God appeared on earth as man because man's nature is made by God to express him, and in man's nature the divine nature could be revealed: for, " all the earth doth worship Thee, the Father everlasting." All creation is a unity and is made to express God and to worship Him and to respond to His life and spirit which is always within it.

No truth concerning the Christian religion has been more neglected and left out of Christian teaching than this truth that GOD IS INCARNATE and yet it was the main purpose of Christ's coming to reveal it. Its neglect has meant a blindness to the presence of God's Holy Spirit in the world, in every human being, in all nature, and in every one of us. " He was in the world and the world was made by Him and the world knew Him not " (St. John 1. 10).

Because we have failed to realise that " the earth is the Lord's and all that is in it " we have used the earth and the land and all material things as if God was not concerned about them, and as if they only existed for our own selfish purposes.

Because we have failed to realise that God's life is in every human being, we have treated our fellow men, not only of our own nation but of other nations and other colour to ourselves, as if they only existed for our purposes, or as if it did not really matter what conditions they lived under, or whether they were educated or not; and yet, " Inasmuch as ye did it not unto one of the least of these my brethren, ye did it not unto Me " (Matthew 24. 45).

Because we have thought that God was far away up in heaven and have not realised that His life and spirit is always within us and, therefore, always adequate to our need, we have lived often and for periods, perhaps every day, as atheists, because we have forgotten Him and lived as if He did not exist: and in consequence we have been worried and been anxious and made ouselves ill and unfit for God's service.

Yet there is no need for all this individual and social failure and sin, nor for the misery and suffering which we see in the world. Christ came to show us the way out. " I am come that they may have life and have it abundantly." " God so loved the world that He gave His only begotten Son to the end that all that believe in Him should not perish but have Life." And yet, still, people are perishing, through sickness and disease, through anxiety and worry, through hunger and war and oppression. It need not be. GOD IS INCARNATE. He is in us and around us always. His life and spirit is in all the world. You can see His life at work if you watch your lawn after you have cut it: or your rose trees when you have pruned them. There is creative life pushing out to repair the damage. If you break your leg, the doctor sets it and puts it into plaster to keep it still, but it is creative life working within which heals the bone. God is above all and through all and in you all (Ephesians 4. 6) all the time and always at work.

The life of God is in every cell of life in all the world and in your body and there is no division between God and nature or between natural and supernatural. The same life works in all, always working to express itself. Creation, however, is not all on the same level and the capacity for the expression of God's life is greater on the higher levels than on the lower. While the beauty of God's life can find expression in the mountains and in the sunrise and in the flowers and trees; that life will find much fuller expression in the higher animals than in the flowers. In the love and care of the mother animal for her offspring we see something of the love of God as we see it also on a still higher plane in the human mother, but our human nature is capable of expressing far more of the love of God than the animal is able to do. It is, in fact, capable of expressing many of the spiritual qualities of God's life and character; His self sacrificing love, joy, peace, goodness, beauty, truth, justice, equity, freedom, wisdom, wholeness and health. Only as we do indeed express or incarnate these qualities, do we become truly human and truly "Sons of God." It is part of the purpose of the Christian life to teach us how to do this.

God, however, is not content to incarnate His life and spirit in us as individuals. There are some of His qualities which could never reach their full expression in isolated human beings. And God is in His own Eternal Being a Trinity in which there is not only an activity of love but variety in unity. We would expect this nature of God to find expression in the fellowship of those who unite in His Spirit. We find this expression in the deepest experiences of human relationships, in really deep friendships and perhaps most of all in the marriage relationship: for in this two people experience and express a unity and love which would be impossible to one alone. "What does he see in her?" or "What does she see in him?" people ask when they hear of an engagement. And truly they see in one another what no one else sees, for they see with the eyes of love, and that is with the eyes of God, what they can be to one another. It is this vision, if kept alive by self sacrificing love, which enables them to enter into the one flesh union in marriage and to be true to one another through the whole of their life: their love for one another deepening as they grow older. In this they incarnate the love of God. A similar incarnation of God's spirit is experienced by those who enter into and share in the family life of the Church where those who worship together become a real "Body of Christ" and enter into a deep fellowship with Him and with one another in the cause of His Kingdom.

In both marriage and in the life of the Church we experience an incarnation which has become a deep spiritual experience which gives us a foretaste of the final incarnation which will be accomplished when God is known in His Creation to be all in all and His Kingdom comes into experience and expression, and that which is physical becomes a true incarnation of the spiritual, for God's Kingdom will have come " on earth as it is in Heaven."

It is this purpose of incarnation which makes the whole creation sacramental: and it is against this background that we must see the sacraments of the Church, for they are the high-lights of the Sacramental Creation, which link up God's purpose for the Church with His purpose in creating the world.


## CHAPTER XXVI

### THE SACRAMENTS

I spoke of the laying on of hands as a " Sacramental Act " in distinction from the sacraments of the Church, the number of which has varied greatly throughout the history of the Church. At various times it has been thought that there were twelve, or even thirty sacraments, and only late in history has the Church come to believe that there are seven sacraments, and of these, two — Baptism and Holy Communion — have been looked on as sacraments through which salvation must be attained.

There has been, and still is, a great lack of understanding about the sacraments, and I think it has arisen from the same cause which led to the loss of the Ministry of healing in the Church.

From the early part of the fourth century, the Church became very transcendental in it's thought of God (see Chapter 8), that is, it thought of God as if He were entirely far away up in Heaven. The result was that it thought less and less of His life being in all creation: and it, therefore, largely lost any thought of creation itself being sacramental, that is, of creation being the means through which God expresses or manifests His life and character and perfection. Creation is made to incarnate God: it is sacramental in nature and purpose, though evil is all the time thwarting God's purpose and much of creation fails to become what God means it to be. It has fallen from the purpose of God.

As a result of this change in theological thought in the fourth and fifth centuries, the sacraments of the Church became separated in thought from creation and, therefore, became isolated, and, to a degree, magical acts. If we are to recover the true meaning of the sacraments and understanding of their great value we must see them as the high-lights of a sacramental creation; that is a creation in which God is always at work, striving to express His eternal and infinite spirit and His character and wholeness in all things: the sacraments being the points at which this is achieved. The whole teaching of the Gospel is the good news that creation has a sacramental purpose and that God intends creation to become His Kingdom on earth, expressing all that is in Heaven. It is against this background that we see the meaning of the sacraments.

*The Sacrament of Holy Baptism* is the way in which we are made members of the Christian Church: but it is much more than this. It deals with human persons who have been made by God as part of His Creation and who are part of the human race for whom Christ has died upon the Cross. Every child born into the world, of whatever race, is a child of God with an element of God's life within him. William Law called this " a seed of Divine Life having within it all the riches of Eternity." Under certain conditions this life or seed can grow and express itself and the child of God can grow into a Son of God, manifesting the fruits of the Spirit. The condition is that he must be brought to know God and His Son Jesus Christ. " This is Life Eternal that they should know Thee the only true God and Him whom Thou didst send, even Jesus Christ " (John 17. 3). " Verily I say unto you he that heareth my word and believeth him that sent me hath eternal life and cometh not into judgment, but hath passed out of death into Life " (John 5. 24).

The child as he is born into the world has the greatest possible potentialities, but he cannot attain to them unless he is brought into his right relationship with God in Christ. This must be done through a new birth or Baptism. Baptism is " regeneration " or a new birth. It is not a new conception: as is so often taught or implied. There is nothing magic about it: but just as a child is conceived and grows in the womb until he can grow no more and then needs to be born into the wider environment of the world, so that his body can develop and grow: so the child of God who is born into this world, finds himself surrounded by the world with all its wrong values and unbelief and sin, is unable to grow and to develop in spiritual ways, and so needs to be born a second time and to pass through the water of Baptism into the wider environment of the fellowship of Christ's Church. By Baptism the child is made a member of Christ's Body, the Church. He is, therefore, as St. Paul says, part of the "flesh and bones" of that Body which "is Christ" (Ephesians 5. A.V.). He is declared to be "the Child of God" by virtue of his incorporation into Christ. And again, being one with Christ, he is an inheritor of all that is in Christ —" an inheritor of the Kingdom of Heaven." Then, as a member of the Body which "is Christ" (1 Corinthians 12. 12), he shares in its fellowship and in all the teaching and spirit and activity of the Christian group or Church. He begins from his earliest days to imbibe and absorb from the fellowship of the Church which is the Spirit filled Body of the risen Christ, the Holy Spirit, and grows up as a Christian, a true Son of God, manifesting His life and character.

This is the meaning of the new birth in Baptism. It is very real, if the Church is truly the Body of Christ and inspired with His Spirit, and not a congregation and nothing more, as is the case so often. The child (or the older person) is transplanted by baptism, as a plant into new and good soil, so that all that is of God in him may grow and blossom and bring forth fruit. He grows up with, and is trained by the members of the fellowship to know his calling and to be responsible for the work of Christ's Church in the world and he looks forward to being a member of Christ, not only in this life, but in that mystical Body of Christ which grows towards "the stature of the fulness of Christ, unto a full grown man" (Ephesians

3. 13), in whom all the children of God will one day find their place beyond death, for only when we wake up after His likeness shall we be satisfied with it (Psalm 17. 15). And in this Body He will come again with Christ and all His Saints at the coming of His Kingdom (1 Thessalonians 3. 13). It is into this universal community in Christ that every Child of God who is ever born into the world is intended by God to come.

It is as we see Baptism against the background of God's purpose in creation that our eyes are opened to its value and its importance and to a wider vision of the greatness of our calling, and of the mission of the Church.

## CONFIRMATION

Baptism is then completed by Confirmation when the member of Christ's Body, having been trained and taught in " the Fellowship," is ordained (or Ordered) by " the laying on of hands " as part of the priestly Body of the Church and given his authority to act in Communion with the Body. To enable him to fulfil this responsibility he is given the gift of the Holy Spirit to strengthen and guide him and to give him wisdom to do God's will and work. Baptism incorporates him into Christ and Confirmation enables him to fulfil his high calling.

This aspect of Confirmation, as the ordination of each lay person who has been baptised into Christ's Church, is often entirely absent from the teaching given in preparation of candidates for Confirmation. The gift of the Holy Spirit is spoken of as if it were quite a new beginning in the Christian life, instead of being the power of God given to the newly ordained member of the Church, who is now made responsible for the work of the Church in which he has grown up. The Church is the priestly Body of Christ and in this priesthood we share. In the Holy Communion, Christ is the Priest and the whole Body shares in His activity, which is always an activity of redemption and of healing and of restoring creation, which has fallen from its true sacramental nature, to what God has made it and intends it to be. Thus in Baptism completed by Confirmation, we have the building up and preparing of the Body which Christ needs if He is to continue His redeeming, healing work in the world, that it may become perfect as His great sacrificial offering to His Father; that which expresses His own eternal perfection, " the Kingdom of God."

## CHAPTER XXVII

### HOLY COMMUNION

The Sacraments need to be seen as the high-lights of a sacramental creation. This, we have seen, was so with Baptism. By creation every child has a seed of divine life within and is a Child of God and potentially a Son of God. In Baptism he is claimed as the Child of God and brought into the Body which " is Christ " and which is responding to His Spirit and which is aware of this relationship to Christ.

So it is with the Holy Communion; all creation and, therefore, all bread and wine, are made by God to be sacramental, but a large part of creation has not become what God meant it to be, it has " missed the mark " and failed to express the glory of God's perfection. It is, in other words, a fallen creation and much of it has been degraded from God's purpose by misuse and by the action of sinful men. Iron and steel, which should have served God's purposes for men, have been degraded into guns and tanks for destruction and tyranny; and bread and wine which should have been shared by the human race in justice and fellowship, have been degraded by man's selfishness and greed, and so some have more than they need and others starve.

Now, God is concerned to put this evil right, that is, to redeem and heal His creation, whatever it may cost Him in suffering. He does it through Jesus Christ and He needs to complete it through Jesus Christ working through His Church which is His Body.

*This is what Holy Communion is about.* It is not just

a service of praise and prayer — it is a " Memorial." " Do this for My memorial," or " do this in memory of Me," or " in remembrance of Me." But this word " memorial " means much more than " in memory of Me." Jesus used the word " Anamnesis." It is a word used in psychology for bringing vividly into the present something that happened in the past and all the feelings connected with it. And this is what Holy Communion is. It brings all that Jesus Christ has been doing from the very beginning to the present. Before creation, Jesus existed; He was the eternal " Word of God," ever giving to His Father the perfect expression of His own being and, therefore, worshipping the Father, in the true sense of worship, giving to the Father that which was worthy of Him.

In creation, the eternal Word continued this worship, when He carried this activity of love into time and space. " All the earth doth worship Thee, the Father everlasting " (Te Deum). This means that the whole creation and all that is within it is made by Christ to be a great offering or sacrament expressing His Father's perfection. This is what Jesus was talking about when He spoke of " the Kingdom of God " coming " on earth as in heaven." (See Chapters 2 and 3). And in the Holy Communion we bring all this activity of Christ, the whole purpose of God for creation, vividly into the present.

What do we do in Holy Communion? We do five things:

1. We gather together as members of Christ to be His Body. We are Christ. He is in us and we in Him. In us Christ is in action through His Body.

2. Christ in us and with us takes bread and wine into His hands; and in doing this, takes a representative part of fallen creation into His hands. Bread and Wine have been through the industrial process. They begin as wheat and grapes and have passed through the labour market of the world with all its sin and selfishness; they have been gambled for on the Stock Exchange and in the wheat pools and are tainted by the sin of

the world. Yet they are part of His creation which was meant to be the sacrament of His Being: and as He is and always has been the Redeemer and Healer of all creation, He takes degraded creation into His hands

3. Christ, then, acting through His Body, the Church, restores creation to its true nature. He breaks the bread, that it may be shared and blesses both bread and wine: and then declares it to be His Body and His Blood — the true outward and visible sign or form of His life within. Here in the broken bread we see the broken Body which hung upon the Cross, and in the wine we see the blood of Christ, the cost of His redemption brought vividly into the present, as was the incarnation when God in Christ took upon Himself the sin and evil of the world and redeemed it by suffering.

This is " our sacrifice of praise and thanksgiving " not only an " anamnesis " or " memorial of His Cross and passion," but of His whole creative, redemptive activity of love from the beginning and for the future. An activity into which we are called to enter.

4. The climax of Holy Communion is when we as a body " offer ourselves, our souls and bodies " to Christ to be His lively Body, responsive to His call and to His will. He then accepts us and fills us with the true sacramental food, the " Bread of Life," which unites us not only to Him but to one another in Him. We " feed on Him in our hearts by faith with thanksgiving." The Church, then, as His Body, is sent forth into the world to be Christ in the world, redeeming it as He always has done and needs to do now through His " lively Body."

5. It is by regular attendance and participation in Holy Communion that a congregation grows into a body and becomes aware of its unity in Christ and learns to have a sense of responsibility to Him for His work in the world.

Any sick members of this body are not only defects in the Body of Christ, but we ourselves are sick in them and responsible for their healing.

Any members of the body who are absent from the gathering of the body are a weakness and need to be brought back.

In the Holy Communion, every time it is celebrated, God's Kingdom comes in the perfecting of bread and wine. We see how Christ changes what is evil and so how He redeems and heals and, those who have eyes to see, see how the world must be redeemed with Christ. The Church tends to become a community filled with purpose and enthusiasm for Christ's Kingdom.

## CHAPTER XXVIII

### HOLY UNCTION

Holy Unction is a sacrament of the Church which has been used for many hundreds of years, but was lost when the Roman Church changed it from a healing sacrament to one of committal before death, or " Extreme Unction " as it is called. It is only recently in the Anglican Church that the revival of its use has begun. It is a sacrament which has its roots in the Gospels and in the earliest practice of the Christian Church. We must, therefore, study its history and the early methods of its ministration. But first, we are considering the Sacraments as the high-lights of Sacramental Creation. In all creation God is working through Christ to express His own perfect life, that all creation may become His Kingdom on earth as in Heaven. In that creation, human beings are made to grow into His likeness as His children. Hence the need for the Church and for baptism into Christ, for cleansing in water, and then for the gift of the Holy Spirit in Confirmation, to enable each member to grow by God's grace into the fulness of Christ's life. In Holy Communion we have the whole scheme of God's redemption brought vividly before us and we ourselves are caught up into it to work with Christ in overcoming evil and in offering the whole creation to the Father as His Kingdom. So in Holy Unction we have a sacrament which brings before us the natural healing work of the Holy Spirit who is always at work on the natural level and lifts it into the sacramental life of the Church, making it the assurance of God's purpose of healing and the pledge which assures us that He is at work. There are many created gifts which aid healing and in our Lord's day oil was used medicinally and it is used still in some cases for healing. How naturally it would become used as the matter of the healing sacrament. But if oil is the matter to be blessed for sacramental use, how important it is that other properties of God's healing, such as penicillin and many other medicines, should be recognised and blessed, for God uses them in His purposes of healing, and has given medical science the wisdom and skill to heal on the natural level, making it one of the channels of His healing purpose for men. It seems likely that Jesus Himself used oil in some of His ministrations and that following His example the disciples also used it, for we are told of the twelve disciples that " they cast out many devils and anointed with oil many that were sick and healed them " (Mark 6. 13).

The sacrament of Holy unction derives from the instructions given in St. James' Epistle, 5. 13-16 : " Is any among you suffering? Let him pray. Is any cheerful? Let him sing praises. Is any among you sick? Let him call for the Elders of the Church; and let them pray over him, anointing him with oil in the name of the Lord : and the prayer of faith shall save him that is sick, and the Lord shall raise him up; and if he has committed sins, they shall be forgiven him. Confess, therefore, your sins one to another, and pray one for another, that ye may be healed."

Father Puller in his book, " Anointing the Sick," published by the S.P.C.K. for the Church Historical

Society, points out that St. James is here speaking of two quite distinct sacraments. First, the anointing of the sick with oil for healing and then the forgiveness of sins. The forgivenes of sins would not necessarily be given before unction, but it would certainly be given if the sick person had committed serious (or mortal) sin, after confession to the Elders of the Church. No forgiveness is conveyed through Unction itself. This was the custom of the Church right up to the end of the seventh century. The practice of anointing the sick was carried on throughout the history of the Church, but no idea of forgiveness being given through this sacrament appears until the reign of Emperor Charles the Great in the year 813 A.D. Forgiveness was given through the Sacrament of Penance, in which the Christian, realising his union and fellowship in the Body of Christ, confessed the sins which he knew had hurt and let down not only God Himself, but all the other members of the Church to which he belonged. The Absolution was the forgiveness of God and of the Fellowship, and this restored the person, not only to fellowship with God, but to the Church. Thus very frequently these two sacraments were used together: the one in preparation for the other.

The oil which was to be used for anointing was blessed by the priest before the final dismissal in the Communion Service. Lay people brought the oil to the altar and generally brought water as well. Both of these were blessed and given back to the lay people and taken by them to the sick person who drank the water and was then anointed, sometimes all over, with the oil. It was not till the year 813 A.D. that the anointing was made by the priest and the ministration confined to the priesthood. This simple, partly medicinal, use of the oil was characteristic of all the early sacramentaries or service books of the Church.

By the year 1100 A.D. Holy Unction had become a Sacrament of forgiveness, and the purpose of healing had gradually been lost; it became the custom in the Western Church to anoint the eyes, ears, nose, mouth, hands, feet, and the reins or kidneys, praying for God's forgiveness for the sins committed through each of these organs of the senses. This was administered just before death with the Viaticum or last Communion. In the year 1551, at the Council of Trent, the Roman Church brought a new sacrament into existence known as " Extreme Unction."

Since the early years of this century, efforts have been made to recover the use of Holy Unction as the Healing Sacrament of the Anglican Church, and also of the Sacrament of Penance without compulsion. These sacraments are now widely used. This has led other parts of the broken Body of Christ to think about the use of this Sacrament and there is hope of its fuller recovery.

Unction is one of the sacraments of the Church and ought to be given to those who are living the sacramental life of the Church and who understand the Church's teaching. It will often be given with the laying on of hands. The service will often either precede or follow the Holy Communion. It is short. The 23rd Psalm is followed by a lesson and prayers. The oil will have been previously blessed by the Bishop who usually blesses oil for the purpose on Maundy Thursday.

The sign of the Cross is made with the oil on the person's forehead with the words, " Name : ————— I anoint thee with this Holy Oil in the name of the Father and of the Son and of the Holy Ghost." Then with hand laid on the head the Priest says, " As with this visible oil thy body has been outwardly anointed so God grant thy soul to be inwardly anointed with the Holy Ghost who is the spirit of all healing, of all strength, of all joy and peace. May He make thee whole in soul and mind and body; release thee from every pain and bondage, through Jesus Christ our Lord." This is followed by thanksgiving and blessing. This service may be repeated at the discretion of the Priest. The usual practice in the Ministry of healing the sick would be to prepare and teach the sick person (as in Chapters 16 and 17), and then to give the laying on of hands (as in Chapter 20). If progress was slow after this, fuller teaching would be given in preparation for the use of the Sacraments of Penance and that of Holy Unction.  Many people who have been seriously ill would testify to the great spiritual strength given in such ministration and to ultimate growth in wholeness.

## CHAPTER XXIX

### EXORCISM OF EVIL SPIRITS

Very few people can speak on this subject in any dogmatic way.  There is no doubt whatever of the power of evil which is widespread in the world and it brings its harvest of suffering and misery.  Only Jesus Himself could say, " The Prince of this world cometh and hath nothing in me."  We pray, in our Lord's prayer, "deliver us from evil," because we are living in a fallen world and we are all involved in its evil and are tight in its grip.  We need to be delivered and only God can do it and lead us out of the darkness into His light.

1.  Psychology has taught us a great deal about the make up and working of man's mind.  We know the unconscious mind is open to the thoughts of those around us and is infected by them.  It also retains memories or records of long consciously forgotten events, with all the emotion connected with them still attached.  This means that our deep unconscious minds are often deeply tainted with the evil of the world and this evil may cause great conflict with high ideals which are also held there from our teaching in early life.  A divided mind on this deep level may cause great emotional strain and lead to mental or nervous breakdown.

2.  There is no doubt that many symptoms which in the past came as expressions of sub-conscious stress, were taken for possession by an evil entity, or as devil possession, but this does not account for every mental condition of illness.

It is, however, important that, in cases where a person

thinks himself to be possessed by an evil spirit, he should be treated as one possessed, for the obsession itself is an evil spirit within him and is very objective to him: and he will only trust a person who believes what he believes, and whom he knows has power and authority to exorcise the evil. A priest who can get beside him in that way may be able to lead him to repentance and confession in preparation for exorcism, which may reveal the evil which has caused the conflict and bring him to acceptance of forgiveness and peace. Exorcism of the evil will then be the sacramental way of bringing him assurance of deliverance from the evil by the grace of God.

3. Again, on the deepest level of the unconscious mind there are, in some people, records of deeply disturbing events with much emotion attached: it may be of hatred, fear, resentment, desire for revenge, sex and so on. We all of us use a great deal of energy to keep these feelings and memories down in the unconscious mind and out of the conscious mind. Circumstances, however, may arise to deplete our nervous energy, over-work, or stress and strain of some kind, and then these emotions tend to come up into our conscious mind and we become obsessed with fears or resentments or desire to hurt, which have no present attachments within our conscious knowledge and these may become quite irrational. "Here is an evil spirit within me — making me want to hurt someone:" or, "Why am I so full of fear that I can't go out alone?" says the patient.

This is an evil spirit which needs to be recognised for what it is and to be dealt with by deep meditation, or perhaps by deep analysis. But again, exorcism can be given and be the sacramental assurance that the power of God's love and forgivingness can reach even the depths of the mind and bring redemption and healing and the casting out of evil by deep change of consciousness.

4. Once again, the mind can learn and come to the pos-session of intuitive knowledge. The larger part of our daily habits and reactions to circumstances are the result of such learning or training. We learn our multiplication

tables when we are small children and to the end of our lives we know that six sixes are thirty-six without having to think about it. We even speak of "one track minds," because we act quite unconsciously, and even think in such a way because of frequent repetition of some way of thought. So also it is possible for people to become possessed by evil habits or negative thoughts. During the war people who were in concentration camps in Germany were obliged to lie consistently for months, in order to hide their Jewish blood or to protect someone else, and the constant habit of lying became an obsession which they could not get rid of when they got their release. They were possessed by the evil habit. What they needed was an assurance of delivery, and this could be given effectively by exorcism of the evil. Many people who have for long thought lightly of evil have found themselves bound by the evil which has taken possession of their wills.

These forms of possession are more frequent than many people realise and the Church has the power and authority to release people from bondage to such evil.

5. There are, however, cases of possession by unknown entities, which seem to be human personalities. The person has opened himself to such possession by making his mind void, or by dabbling in spiritualism. There are evil personalities who having loved this world and its evil, are earth bound and have no desire to progress after death, and desire to return to the earth. In certain conditions they are able to take possession of people who are open to such possession. The number of such cases is probably not large in this country, but more frequent in pagan countries, where black magic is practised and evil is encouraged and revered.

These evil spirits can be exorcised: but it is not something which inexperienced people should undertake lightly for they may meet with great opposition from the possessing entity and may themselves become affected by the evil.

The Priest who intends to help a person who is "possessed" must prepare himself carefully. He would do well to make his own confession in which he will confess not only his own individual sins but his own involvement in the evil of the world and of his nation. His acceptance of absolution and forgiveness will give him an assurance of his restoration to and unity with the Body of Christ whose prayers he will need. He will be fortunate if he practises regularly the method of contemplative meditation, for then he will renew his consciousness of complete unity with Christ in what he is about to do. He will have lost all self consciousness and fear and know the power of the crucified Risen Christ who " by the finger of God " casts out devils and brings the eternal life of God's Kingdom into action for healing. He will be a wise minister, who not only prays in this way and prepares himself by fasting also, but who enlists the help of another minister to assist him, and who will be prepared to take over the ministry if he himself becomes tired. For once exorcism begins, there must be no end till the evil spirit has departed.

Successful exorcism will depend a great deal on whether or not the person is willing and desirous of being healed and is co-operative. There are, in ordinary illness, compensations for illness. A person may have found illness a very convenient way of escape from unwanted responsibility. So a person who is possessed may have found great kindness and even protection in his illness and he may be unwilling to abandon this. The patient, therefore, will need a good deal of preparation, during which the minister will teach and inspire him with a desire for freedom and progress in living, through the power of Christ. During this time the minister will be careful to be very positive in all that he says, and to refrain from criticism of what may seem absurd or wrong ideas, taking these as the symptoms of an unhinged mind. Criticism or any direct rebuke of such ideas as being untrue would be met quickly by antagonism, which would hinder all progress. In all contact with such cases, we must be very aware that Christ is within each one of us, not two Christs, but one, and to be aware of His love and power at work overcoming all evil and untruth. " Now ye are the Body of Christ and members in particular . . . are all workers of miracles? Have all gifts of healing? . . . Yet show I unto you a more excellent way. Though I speak with the tongues of men and of angels and have not love I am nothing . . . Love is not easily provoked . . . love never faileth " (1 Corinthians 12 and 13).

It is Christ Himself who is at work through His Body the Church, and never for a moment must we forget it. Suggested forms for exorcism are supplied by the Guild of Health, 26 Queen Anne Street, W.1, on application.

### After Care

It is most important that anyone who has been afflicted mentally by the power of evil and has been ministered to by exorcism and healing, should be helped by the Church for some time and until full rehabilitation has been achieved.

This will be aided most by fellowship within a Christian Group where there is real love between the members and a spirit of prayer.

If the person is not confirmed he ought to be given instruction, in preparation for confirmation and full membership of His Church.

He will also be greatly helped by being taught to meditate every day and by being led on to contemplative meditation in which he will find the way to a deeper knowledge of God in his own experience. For unless his experience of God becomes greater than his past experience of evil, he is in danger of relapse. He ought, therefore, to be included in the prayers of other praying members of the Church, and deeply cared for by them.

# CHAPTER XXX
## SUFFERING

We must not confuse suffering with evil: it is not the same problem. It is true that some suffering is due to evil, but not all suffering is evil. It is for our benefit that we suffer if we put our hand into the fire, it warns us ơi danger: it is like a red light. It is for our benefit that a diseased appendix gives agonising pain, for it brings the doctor to perform an operation without which we would probably die. In these and other ways, suffering acts like a tutor, it teaches us and has an educational purpose or it warns us of danger or of something that needs our immediate attention, like a thorn in the flesh. For suffering of this kind we may well give God thanks. But all suffering is not of this kind. The world is very out of harmony with God, and the result is widespread evil in which we are all involved and evil brings much suffering: some undeserved and some which we know we deserve. The truest thing which we can say of this suffering is that it can be used, either well or badly. It can harden a person who refuses to accept it or tries to escape it, it may lead him to blaspheme and to be bitter: on the other hand it can be faced and accepted and entered into with Christ and used for the glory of God, and then it will sift and test the sufferer and soften him and he will be able to bring great good out of it for his own soul and for the help of others. And yet, it is not sent by God, because suffering is not an entity in itself, there is no such thing as suffering apart from a cause, any more than there is evil by itself. It is a symptom of evil expressing itself in suffering, just as evil expresses itself in a hydrogen bomb, or in the iron nails of the Cross or in sickness and disease. Sin takes form in a multitude of ways. It pours forth in speech in cursing, it is built into bricks and mortar in slums. So suffering as in all these and other manifestations of sin and evil must never be separated from the thought of its cause, and God, whose purpose of goodness has been turned to evil, is always working to overcome the evil and to restore all things to the perfection which He wills. And God can only overcome this evil as He did the evil which turned on him in Christ as He challenged it during his incarnate life. He took it upon Himself and refused to give it any new life in Himself; and without hatred or resentment or desire to punish, He suffered it and ended it and redeemed it by His love and in so doing incarnated the love of God. And as He is now in all the world and in us and in all mankind, He still bears the sin of the world and calls us to share it with Him when it touches us and we suffer. Thus we can share in His redemptive love for men and manifest that love to others as we unite ourselves to Him in fighting and overcoming both sin and suffering.

Now here we must distinguish clearly between two kinds of suffering. There is a vocation to suffering for Christians, but not to every kind of suffering. A great deal of suffering is the direct or indirect result of sin. We may be involved in the sin of our nation and suffer the horrors of war, or we may be suffering from sickness which so often has a background of evil of which we are unconscious. God does not want war or sickness or any suffering that comes from evil. And we ourselves do not voluntarily want to suffer in this way. There is no vocation to this kind of suffering and we do right to seek healing and peace for ourselves and for the world. We do right in going to the doctor. If suffering of this kind comes we can only try to bring as much good out of it as we can and realise that Christ suffers it all with and in us. We may then try to enter into fellowship with Him, as He bears the sin of the world still and offer ourselves to serve Him in challenging the evil and overcoming it. It is His Cross not ours. It is His Will to heal and to end it.

But there is another kind of suffering to which every Christian is called. It is the suffering which comes when we oppose evil and refuse to have our part in it. This may bring physical suffering, even imprisonment and death; it may bring loss of friends and misunderstanding.

It may bring loss of promotion in our profession. It may bring very great hurt to our minds and feelings: but this is suffering for righteousness sake. This is the suffering which our Lord Jesus suffered on the Cross. It is blessed in the Beatitudes: and Christ calls us to take up our Cross and follow Him and we are all too slow to do so. " Ye are the salt of the earth " (Matthew 5. 13) and salt ought to paralyse the corruption of the world. We are brought up in a Christian home and country and we have all been slightly salted by our Christian teaching, but that is not enough, we are called to *be* salt, to challenge evil. If we do so we will suffer and Christ expects us to be prepared to do so. It is in this suffering that we take up our Cross.

It is important that we should be clear that the teaching of the Old Testament on suffering is entirely different to that of the New Testament. Our Lord quite clearly corrected the Jewish attitude to suffering. In the Old Testament, pain was thought of as a punishment. But that idea was an overhang from paganism. Abraham did not come quite suddenly to a full understanding of the true religion. He was a pagan and he came to believe in the God of Righteousness, but he still believed that God wanted human sacrifice and he was ready to sacrifice Isaac; but he learned the truth in his obedience. There are many pagan ideas in the Old Testament which were only slowly left behind as time went on. The Bible is not only God's revelation and Word to us, it is also the history of man's growing understanding of God as he searches for the truth and learns by experience. So the Jews thought of God punishing sinners and of His wrath and vengeance upon them. They had not yet seen God taking the sin of the world upon Himself and dealing with it by suffering it upon the Cross. So Job, in Chapter 19, cries out against God who has afflicted him and in Chapter 7 against God's punishment. In Psalms 88 and 90 we see the Jewish idea of God. Archbishop Temple wrote of the latter " splendid stoicism but not Christian." The idea of suffering being punishment for sin persisted to our Lord's day. He was asked (Luke 13. 1-5) about the Galileans whose blood Pilate had mingled with their sacrifices. " Think ye that these Galileans were sinners above all others, because they suffered these things? I tell you Nay." And of the eighteen killed by the fall of the Tower of Siloam, " think ye that they were offenders above all men? I tell you Nay." The Jews would have said " Yes " to each question. And in John IX His disciples asked about the man who was born blind, " Who did sin, this man or his parents?" The Jews would have said either the man had sinned or his parents. But Jesus says, " Neither did this man sin nor his parents. But that the works of God should be made manifest in him, we must work the works of Him that sent me while it is day," and He then healed him. This is a similar answer to those given in Luke 13 above. It is a denial of the idea that suffering is punishment. " The works of Him that sent me " was obviously to be seen in healing and Jesus immediately healed the man. But, you will notice I have changed the stops in the quotations. Greek, in which language the Gospels were written, has no stops: they have to be put in by the translators and here they seem to have been put in the wrong place which altered the sense of what Jesus was saying. It is, therefore, necessary to correct them. Christ came to end sickness and suffering by ending sin and evil. " When I am in the world I am the light of the world," and when he had said that He healed the blind man. For this reason also in Luke 13 he said, " Except ye repent ye shall all likewise perish," because sin brings suffering upon ourselves.

It is in Christ on the Cross that we see most clearly the way in which suffering can be met and used to the glory of God. He had seen the power of evil manifested in sickness—" This woman whom Satan hath bound " (Luke 13. 16). He knew that it would test his own loyalty, " The Prince of this world cometh and hath nothing in me " (John 14. 30). Evil did its worst but found no response to evil in Him and so He ended and redeemed it and showed us how to do likewise in God's strength.

# CHAPTER XXXI

## THE SUFFERER

It was important to get our ideas about suffering straight in the last Chapter but for those who suffer, something more is needed.

Severe pain, and specially long endured and wearing pain, can bring great desolation and great temptation to forget that God is within us and to become self-centred and so to lose hope of overcoming in His strength.

God is in the midst of us; He is also within us; He is bearing the pain with us. Christ has been crucified from the foundation of the world. He suffers in all the suffering of creation (Matthew 25. 31-46; and 10. 29; and Hebrews 2. 18). And so He is with us sharing it all. "Underneath are the everlasting arms." The help we need is within us and it is adequate to our need.

Besides this, God is at work to overcome the evil which causes suffering and it is His will to end the suffering, because His will is perfection for His whole creation. Unless we know this deeply we will be looking all the time for outside help alone.

The suffering may be either mental or physical. It may be the deep grief of unrequited love or of separation from someone we love, or of failure through our own fault. On the other hand it may be unrelieved agony of physical pain, long endured.

In either case the fact of suffering which comes from and is a symptom of disharmony and evil — perhaps quite undeserved — does lay us open to very great temptation, which if it is given way to, increases our suffering and bars the way to relief.

The temptation is to self-centredness, because we are inevitably alone in our suffering unless God is very real to us. The temptation is to forget Him and to become entirely concerned to find a remedy for relief from pain, and for this to become an obsession. Nothing hinders healing more than this. And yet, we must not blame those who are driven to it, it is so real a danger and such a hard struggle to overcome. It is so easy to crave sympathy and even to resent not getting it, and even to fear owning up to slight improvement in our condition, in case we should lose sympathy. As I look back to many wonderful cases of healing through deep faith and trust in God, I don't remember one that took place till this struggle with self was faced, and God became the centre; not " let me be relieved of this pain and that I may be healed of this illness "— but " that I may serve God and glorify Him in it and in whatever comes. God is good and His will is always perfect, I can trust Him."

When we are weak and low-spirited our powers of resistence to evil are weakened and it is so easy to seek sympathy from friends and to depend on it. Then, if we don't get it, or don't get as much as we think we ought to get we become lonely and isolated and we may even become resentful and when someone comes to see us we thrust our misery upon them trying to make them suffer with us, because we can't bear the isolation which suffering brings and which they are not sharing with us.

The only remedy is to get our heart right with God. When we are sure of Him, our heart will sing, even in pain. God does not promise us an easy life but He does promise that He will never leave us and we know that His grace is sufficient for us.

Our Lord suffered great pain upon the Cross and with it He experienced the loneliness of suffering when He cried, " My God, my God, why hast Thou forsaken me?" The utter dereliction and forsakenness and isolation which comes with great pain is a severe test of our whole prayer life and faith as it was for Him. If that is deeply based on the goodness of God; if our knowledge of Him is intuitive, then, like Jesus, our cry will be " My God, my God." If it isn't we shall curse like the dying thief or drift into self pity which will rob us of the only help which can come, that of knowing our unity with Christ in His Cross. It is in this unity with Christ that we get outside of self and in the experience of some get outside of the pain and know His peace : not that we lose the pain, but we are able to put it in the background.

It is, of course, difficult for someone who is in great pain to begin to know this deep unity with Christ. The rain and the storm has come and if our house is built on the sand it may be swept away. We need to be prepared by faithful and persevering meditation (as taught in Chapters 14 and 15) to know the reality of God's life within us. If we do know this, we will gradually become aware of His power in our daily lives : we train ourselves to speak to Him naturally and often. We learn to walk with Him in the street. Then if sickness comes we are not overwhelmed with fear; if pain suddenly attacks us we don't meet it with negative thoughts and expectation of evil. We know Christ's healing power within and thank Him for it. When accidents happen we meet them positively by asking God's forgiveness for our carelessness and expressing our confidence in His healing. Yes, and it comes. Fear always increases the damage done by a cut or a bruise or a burn. This is something which can be proved but it needs great perseverance in meditation to train ourselves to turn to God before we give way to fear or self pity. If we could only learn to take our Lord at His word and believe that what He has told us is true we would find that His presence is real and His power and grace are sufficient for our every need. The world puts limits to what is possible. It talks of evil as inevitable, it looks for the worst. It calls certain diseases "incurable " and in doing so, not only denies the reality but also the power of God. It meets hatred with hatred. It does so because it doesn't know God. He is not real to people who speak in that way. And how often we have got into the habit of talking like this and even believing it. Then when sudden illness or a sudden accident comes, all this negative attitude comes out; we are filled with self pity and fear and we express all the negative attitudes of the world and magnify the evil and often darken our whole outlook before we even being to think of God. It hinders all the healing power of God within us and makes it more difficult for us to recover. It need not be so, and if we take the trouble to learn to know God more deeply, we will find Him adequate to our need.

Jesus, suffering with me and in me, now; let Thy strength be my strength, to Thy glory.


## CHAPTER XXXII

### THE BROKEN BODY OF CHRIST

" Physician heal thyself " (Luke 4. 23). The Church of Christ: His very Body, is broken and divided and very sick. Christ Himself is crucified afresh by us all and let us admit it honestly, we are most of us very little concerned about it.

Our Lord prayed —" that they may all be one; even as Thou Father art in Me and I in Thee, that they may be one in us; that the world may believe that Thou didst send me. And the glory which Thou has given me I have given unto them; that they may be one even as we are one; I in them and Thou in me, that they may be perfected into one; that the world may know that Thou didst send me " (John 17. 21-23). And the purpose which our Lord had was " that the love wherewith Thou lovedst me may be in them and I in them " (John 17. 26). The Church was to be the continuation of the incarnation, the Body in which the love of God could be manifested to the world. It is this manifestation, which is missing from the life of the Church in the world, which hinders people from knowing Christ and seeing Him in the Church. People cannot say as they did in the Early Church, " see how these Christians love one another " (Acts). This is an insuperable hindrance to the missionary and evangelistic work of the Church. We must become concerned about the re-union of the Church or know that we are responsible for the continuance of this treatment of our Lord and its effect on the Church's world wide work.

There is an invisible unity between those who are in Christ, whether they be members of His Body by Baptism, or merely as branches of Him as the vine, and so many people are content with this and have forgotten that Jesus wills His Church to be one in true love for one another as a witness to the world. People ask sometimes, " What is the will of God and how can I do it?" And here it is: His will is that His Church may be one and that all the people of the world shall be brought into it. We may go on from this to say that this united Church is to be the means of bringing the good news of God's purpose to overcome all evil and to establish His Kingdom on earth to all nations.

How has the Church become divided? We must consider this question if we are to see the way back to unity. There were, of course, tensions within the Church from the beginning: even the disciples themselves quarelled about who was the greatest among them: and the first centuries were marked by disputes about doctrine, but even though there was not full agreement the Church held together: it was very loathe to exclude any from the fold, even heretics. As we have seen (Chapter VIII), during the fourth and fifth centuries the Church's idea of God became largely paganised: it began to think that God was entirely transcendent or up in Heaven, and as a result it lost the purpose of redeeming the world. The Church became an ark of salvation conveying the elect over the waves of this troublesome world to a haven in Heaven, beyond the skies. This world became looked upon as " a vale of tears," and the purpose of changing it and cleansing it, and of bringing God's Kingdom from heaven to earth, was forgotten. The Church ceased to have a sacramental purpose of redemption for the world and its whole attention became turned in on itself as an organisation for preparing souls for heaven. This is not the place to outline the process of division which followed. Without the over-all purpose of world redemption there was nothing but self concern to hold the Church together. The Gospel was no longer preached as Christ taught it. It was no longer the good news of God's Kingdom: men were no longer called to the service of Christ's Kingdom and to heal the dis-eases of the world, but to the salvation of individual souls for heaven. God was far away, now and then breaking into the world, intervening by miracles. Prayer aimed at changing His cruel will and jealous disposition by begging and appealing to an unwilling deity who was to be feared and propitiated. No wonder the Church broke up, while the Roman Church tried, and yet tries, to hold a large part of what was the Church together by fear of the tyrannous God in Heaven, and only does so by failing to be Catholic in the only true sense, knowing God as " all and in all," and holding the whole Church in unity. (The word " Catholic " is composed of two Greek words, " kata," according to: and " holos," the whole.)

How can we heal the Body of Christ? Well, of course, we can't do so, only God can do it, and short cuts are useless. We would make greater progress if we could realise that receiving communion together is the crown and the expression of union and love and not the means to it. There may be a good deal of friendliness in a group of people of different denominations who make communion together, but they still remain denominationalists, and some of them only enter into it by denying what their own Church teaches, and do, on a small scale, what would cause further division if it were wider spread.

The first steps to reunion must be repentance and humility in all parts of the Church and acknowledgement that we have all fallen from the fulness of truth as taught by Christ and practised in the Early Church. (1) In our knowledge of God and of His Son Jesus Christ and of the Holy Spirit. (2) In our knowledge of the immanence of His transcendence in all the world and in man. (3) In the knowledge of the Kingdom of God as God's purpose for Creation. (4) In the knowledge of the Holy Spirit at work on both the natural and the supernatural level. (5) In the knowledge of the Church as the Sacramental Body of Christ and the means of our Lord's continued incarnation.

(6) In our readiness to meet people from other parts of the Church frequently to discuss these questions.

If such groups were multiplied widely, the day could come when re-union could be approached by a ten year period of consultation, by opening the councils of the Church to people of differing loyalties for conference and promotion of friendship. This could be followed by discussion on higher levels in the Church, including questions of authority and organisation. Following this there could be a further period with authority given for invitations from one Church to another and at last for an agreement about inter-communion and what is needed for its fulfilment in all Churches. The re-united Church would not then be a surrender to one part of the Church, but a united Catholic Church into which all had brought the riches of their experience and of their love.

The thing that all Christians of all denominations have in common today whenever they meet is the faith which they have in God and in Jesus Christ as Saviour. Isn't this a sufficient basis of unity for us to begin to meet one another in love?

## CHAPTER XXXIII

### DEATH

It comes to every one of us: and it is unlikely that we will not at some time experience it in the death of someone whom we love. What happens? Where do we go? What will there be beyond death? These are questions which we all ask at times.

Jesus did not tell us a great deal about death, though he told us enough to take fear from us. He was much more concerned to teach us the purpose of life, and to know His Father and to call us into union and fellowship with Himself in serving the cause of His Father's Kingdom, than to fix our eyes on death or on any future rewards. The only way of saving our souls is by losing self and becoming absorbed in God's service. God's purpose for us is the same as His purpose for all creation that we may grow into His likeness and in that way glorify Him. God's life is in all creation; on the natural level always working to express itself in a multitude of ways, in flowers in beauty, in birds in song, in animals in still higher forms of life, and in man, in human character, which at its best did express God in Jesus. Creation is progressive and when we have lived out our full span of life on earth, it is normal for our natural faculties to begin to slow down and then to fade away as we go on into the next span of life. The trees do this on a lower level of life. They live out their full span of life and then the sap is withdrawn and the tree puts on its autumn tints and then drops off its leaves, which it needs no longer, and goes on into the winter during which it prepares the buds which it will need when it puts on the glory of the spring. " As the days of a tree shall be the days of my people " (Isaiah 65. 22). We have our chance in this life of growing like God and of becoming His children in the fullest sense and of serving Him. Life is a testing time.

It is true that we are greatly hindered in this aim by the sin and evil of the world by which we are surrounded and in which we are involved. But there is, in every one of us, an awareness of good and evil and a power to choose. God has not left Himself without witness, even to those who have never had a chance of being taught the full truth. His Holy Spirit is in man on the natural level and man can respond to the best that he knows, and in doing so responds to God. But sin may lead us to reject the good and choose evil, and if so, we deteriorate and fall from God's purpose. Life is thus a testing time and when death comes it will find us as we have made ourselves by our choice. At death we drop off the physical body, and having no longer any means of expressing ourselves, we cease to be visible, and enter into the life beyond death and begin at once to progress towards that life of union with God, through Christ, for which God has made us.

Death does not change us in any way. We shall be, five minutes after death, exactly what we were five minutes before death: but our surroundings will be different. We have been told very little of what happens, but in a flash of understanding we will know what we have been and how we have lived, and what is God's purpose and whether we are fit to go on towards it or not. That will be our judgment. Just as you know, in a moment, whether the cake you take out of the oven is good or not: whether the thing you have made as a present for someone is worthy of him or not, so we judge all that we do: and we shall judge ourselves when we wake at death to the truth as it is in Christ. And if we have never responded to the good that we have seen and have constantly chosen evil, we will want to creep away and hide ourselves, for we will be in the hell we have made for ourselves. On the other hand, who can say that when he wakes at death he will be satisfied? The Psalmist is right. " When I wake up after His likeness I will be satisfied with it " (Psalm 17. 15) and not till then. We will none of us be fit to go on to the union with God which He plans for us, and we will all be at different stages of development. Our Lord has given us an inkling. " In My Father's House are many mansions. If it were not so I would have told you " (John 14. 2). After death and judgment we may begin to progress and to learn and we shall find ourselves on a pilgrimage on which there are many resting places or stages (the true meaning of " mansions ") according to our need.

It may be that we have turned away to hell. But hell is not a place, it is a condition; we realise that we have failed and sinned and now we are blind to goodness and isolated and alone with self, humiliated and hopeless. We just don't know how God deals with such souls, but we do know that God is love and never anything else, and that is enough for us to know. " Faithful is the saying . . . that Christ Jesus came into the world to save sinners; of whom I am chief " (1 Timothy 1. 15). Not one of us will be ready to go on. We shall be for a time in Paradise, the state in which souls wait and grow and are cleansed. The dying thief was promised that he would meet Jesus in Paradise (Luke 23. 43), and Jesus Himself went there (1 Peter 3. 19). What has our Lord taught us about the life towards which we progress after death? He said, " I am the Vine and ye are the branches " (John 15. 5). Every single person who has ever come into this world has come out of Christ and all those who live now or ever will live, come out of Him. Mankind is in Jesus: and we all draw our humanity from Him. In Him we hung upon the Cross and were redeemed by Him, for He bore the sin of the world in Himself and triumphed over it. And His will is to gather all mankind to Himself to make the great sacramental Body of His Church, which is not only His Body on earth, but also His Mystical Body in which we all have our places as branches of the Vine and are potential members now. St. Paul speaks of this Body into which we are baptised: " There is one Body and one Spirit even as also ye were called in one hope of your calling; one Lord, one faith, one baptism, one God and Father of all, who is over all, and through all and in all " (Ephesians 4 and 5). And he goes on to point out how Christ has appointed members of this Body with special functions, for the perfecting of the saints, and for the building up of the body till we all attain unto the unity of the faith and of the knowledge of Christ " unto a full grown man, unto the measure of the stature of the fulness of Christ." This whole passage (Ephesians 4. 1-16) should be studied, for here, I believe, we have a vision of God's purpose for us; not only for this world, but for after death as well, when every baptised person will find himself in his place in this Body of Christ and every soul of every nation on earth has also a place waiting to be filled. Jesus said, " I go to prepare a place for you that where I am ye may be also " (John 14. 2), and it will be in this Body — it will be this " full grown Man " who will return with His saints to what Isaiah saw, " the new heaven and the new earth " (Isaiah 65. 17) of His Kingdom, to reign and to be the glory of His Father for ever. Death is not something to be feared by those who sincerely seek to do God's will. It is part of the great adventure of the Christian life, a penalty for sin it is true, but by the victory of Christ's resurrection it is the gateway to life in God's Kingdom.

# CHAPTER XXXIV
## DOCTOR CLERGY CO-OPERATION

Any Priest or Minister who understands something of the causation of illness and disease and of the way in which such causes can be healed by spiritual methods, and in that way health be restored, will find people coming to him for help. He will inevitably be asked the question, " Ought I to continue with my doctor's advice and treatment?" And in almost every case the reply will be, " Yes, of course; medical science is one of the channels through which God works, giving help which is needed on the physical level. Go on doing all that your doctor tells you to do and thank God for his help and pray that God may give him wisdom in his work." Only very rarely will we find an obviously incompetent doctor and then a change of doctor would be indicated and not any disparagement of medical science. Nearly everyone who is ill needs some physical help and some need much more than others. A wise rule for any Christian who is helping a sick person, is to refuse to help anyone who refuses to be under medical care as well as having spiritual help and advice. Our ministry very seldom clashes in any way with that of the doctor.

This cannot be said as wholeheartedly about psychological help. It might be said that a good psychologist will use his psychological knowledge equally well, whether he is a Christian or not: as we would say that a physician or surgeon would do his best to help a person apart altogether from his religious convictions. But psychologists are brought into closer consideration of emotional factors and with religious beliefs and it is more difficult for them to be neutral in their attitudes. When a psychiatrist advises a girl in her early twenties who is disturbed by frequent masturbation, " to go and find a man who will satisfy her:" or a child of ten years old, who tells the psychiatrist that she is having help through prayer, is told,

121

" You mustn't think that that can help you, that is all nonsense," or a woman's suffering from a very serious anxiety neurosis is told that she is " a very bad case and will probably never be any different:" then you can say that these are bad psychologists. But such cases are too frequent to give one the confidence which one ought to have in psychologists who are not Christians. A Christian psychologist will bring with him Christian hope: God's life is working in his patient and he will know that if that life can be released into fulness of life, nothing is impossible.

It has been my happy experience to be a member of a family in which there have been several christian doctors and nurses. I have also known many christian doctors and psychiatrists, some of whom have asked me to help some of their patients and many who undertake their work in a deep spirit of trust in God, and in love for their patients and who realise very fully that they serve God in their fellow men. There is, however great need for deeper Christian understanding in the help that is given to the sick both by doctors and psychologists. Psychology has taught us to understand the importance of the unconscious mind and the devastating effects of what is stored up in it can have upon the body and the mind. But in spite of all the teaching of psychosomatics this has not yet gone deeply into the minds of many doctors. Think for a moment of the number of diseases that are spoken of as " incurable " and the psychological effect of this on the patient and his friends in terms of fear despair discouragement and even of expectation of certain death creeping on: all of these are emotions which will be repressed into the unconscious mind and may be the actual cause of death. The unconscious mind is susceptible to suggestion and will act on it. How many cases of cancer die of fear and of hopelessness in the unconscious mind? Far more, I believe, than of the disease itself. A Christian doctor should be filling his patient's mind with hope: not promising recovery, but assuring him that God's life is in him and is always working to redeem and to overcome evil, for as He is whole and holy, His purpose is to make all things whole and holy. If a doctor did this, he would be helping his patient in a therapeutic way.

It is here that doctor and priest should be working together knowing how involved we all are in the evil of the world, and that God's purposes can be hindered. There is no promise given that we shall be immune from the evil of the world, but we can be certain that God works and can be trusted, *whatever comes.* How we need to teach people to understand the importance of the unconscious mind: that there are in every one of us two quite distinct levels of consciousness. The conscious level of consciousness at which we live our daily life, do our work, are kind and sociable with other people, forgiving and happy, enjoying life: and all this is quite real and sincere. But deep down in the unconscious mind there is another level of consciousness of which we may be quite unaware: some circumstances of deep fear in childhood, some experience of cruelty, a father beating his wife, or even hearing or seeing some obscenity: experiences of which we can have no memory and for which there is no blame. Yet attached to the memory of the event is all the emotion which was then experienced, and quite suddenly under some strong emotion, this consciousness, or just the emotion attached to it, comes to the surface of the mind in a terrible fear, or a desire to kill, or a bitter sense of hatred and resentment, or even a sudden almost uncontrollable erotic desire. We wonder if we are going mad. We have not realised that we can be two entirely different persons; we are not whole, because we have never realised the need for the healing of this deep unconscious mind into which all the evil of life and all its scepticism and unbelief and fear has been pouring ever since we were born.

Doctors, Psychiatrists, Clergy, please when will you combine to help us to be whole?

This needs something much deeper than deep analysis. It needs a deep spiritual purging through prayer and very deep meditation and repentence. This is the Church's part in healing.

# CHAPTER XXXV

## GOD CALLS, WHO WILL ANSWER?

The ministry of healing is not a lost or mislaid part of the Church's ministry. It will not be recovered by a revival of the use of Holy Unction in every parish: nor by holding healing services in every Church, nor by the multiplication of " Healers " with special gifts. It is an essential part of God's whole redeeming purpose for creation, the overcoming of evil of every kind in order that God's purpose of perfection may be achieved for the whole creation and His Kingdom come on earth as it is in Heaven.

It is, therefore, and must become obviously, the activity of the living crucified and risen Christ through His Body the Church. As He preached the Kingdom of God and healed; so today must He be able to do, through His whole Church. Without it there is no Gospel. The world is perishing in misery for lack of it. Without it there is no hope for the world and no meaning in it, no purpose in life; we are merely drifting to disaster.

With the vision of God's purpose for creation, and a way of life leading to it; with the values and principles of the Kingdom given to us in the righteousness of God's character: love, justice, freedom, equity, peace, joy, goodness, fulness of life: we have *THE WAY* and in the presence of the Christ Himself within us, we have the certain power of forgiveness for our sins and of the adequacy of His strength as we serve Him in and with our fellow men.

Communism has a vision of a classless society, of freedom and justice and equity for all men and races. It has caught this vision from Judaism, through the teaching of Karl Marx, who was a Jew. It is this promise of an end to the poverty and exploitation and imperialism of

124

the world which attracts the hungry and oppressed people of the world. But Communism believes that all this can be achieved by man himself. It is blind to the evil of the world as it has affected and weakened man's nature in sin. The Communist idea of man is inhuman and unchristian. It fails to see the sinfulness of man which defeats all his endeavours for a righteous world order: and so fails to see the need of a redeemer and a saviour. Man, if he fails to be a friend of the Communist state, can be liquidated and destroyed as an enemy. Not only does God not exist but there are no lasting or eternal principles of morality. Truth does not exist and all is at the will of expediency. This makes Communism incapable of anything but of reducing human beings to cogs in an inhuman system in which all freedom has disappeared.

Let us go back to the third Isaiah's vision of God's Kingdom, his " way of life " coming on earth (Isaiah 65. 17-end), *For, behold, I create new heavens and a new earth: and the former things shall not be remembered, nor come into mind.* When Heaven, God's life, comes to earth, as we pray for it in the Lord's Prayer: the earth will be so perfect and so different from the world we live in now that this nightmare will be no more remembered. *But, be ye glad and rejoice for ever in that which I create: for behold, I create Jerusalem a rejoicing and her people a joy.* Isaiah sees the Kingdom coming locally. Abraham had been told that it was all nations which were to be blessed. *And I will rejoice in Jerusalem and joy in my people: and the voice of weeping shall be no more heard in her, nor the voice of crying.* When the Kingdom comes there will be no more misery and no more bereavement to cause crying. *There shall be no more thence an infant of days, nor an old man that hath not filled his days: for the child shall die an hundred years old and the sinner being an hundred years old shall be accursed.* Children die in the world today of disease: and illness claims both young and old because of the disharmony and evil of the world; but it will not be so in God's Kingdom: life will be lived out to its fullest span, death will be done away. *And they shall build houses and inhabit them and they shall plant vineyards and eat the fruit of them. They shall not build and another inhabit; they shall not plant and another eat.* Today those who build luxurious houses often live in slums; and those who grow the food of the world are often hungry themselves. There will be no such exploitation and injustice in God's new heaven and new earth. *For as the days of a tree shall be the days of my people and my chosen shall long enjoy the work of their hands.* A tree goes on living from one span of life to another; spring, summer, autumn; it then throws off its leaves and goes on into winter, when it prepares to start the next span of life in the spring. *They shall not labour in vain, nor bring forth for calamity; for they are the seed of the blessed of the Lord and their offspring with them.* The dull useless labour imposed on so many people in the world and the tragic hopelessness of the refugee parents will be no more, for all men will be God's children and brothers in God's family. *And it shall come to pass that, before they call I will answer; and while they are yet speaking, I will hear.* God will be with them and in them and God knows what they need before they ask. Then Isaiah sees in his vision that even the natural order is to be redeemed. *The wolf and the lamb shall feed together and the lion shall eat straw like the ox and dust shall be the serpent's meat.* There, he can't see as clearly in detail: but "nature, red in tooth and claw" doesn't reflect the nature of God, as creation will do in God's Kingdom and of one thing he is sure. *They shall not hurt nor destroy in all my Holy Mountain, saith the Lord.* What a vision! And Christ took up this teaching and that of other O.T. Prophets and based all his teaching about the Kingdom on it. The Christian message to the world is this good news of God's loving purpose for the whole human race: and to be a Christian means that we are called to work with Christ to achieve it. "Go, preach the Kingdom of God and heal the sick."

We need *Clergy* who will be preachers of the Kingdom.

*Theologians* who will study and recover the Gospel.

*Politicians* who will stand by its principles.

*Industrialists* who will put it into practice.

*Homes* which are a foretaste of its spirit.

*A Church* which will " seek first the Kingdom of God and His righteousness." Then " all will be added." The necessities of life, healing, peace. He that hath ears to hear, let him hear.